EMPTY CRADLE

EMPTY CRADLE

DIANA WALSH

DUNDURN
TORONTO

Editor: Matt Baker
Design: Courtney Horner
Printer: Webcom

Library and Archives Canada Cataloguing in Publication

Walsh, Diana, 1959-
      Empty cradle / Diana Walsh.

 Issued also in electronic format.
ISBN 978-1-4597-0657-6

      1. Walsh, Shelby--Kidnapping, 2008. 2. Walsh, Diana, 1959- 3. Hill, Karen Susan. 4. Kidnapping--Ontario--Burlington. 5. Mothers of kidnapped children--Canada--Biography. 6. Female offenders--Biography. 7. Trials (Kidnapping)--Ontario--Milton. I. Title.

HV6604.C32W35 2012   364.15'40971353   C2012-903234-4

1   2   3   4   5   16   15   14   13   12

We acknowledge the support of the **Canada Council for the Arts** and the **Ontario Arts Council** for our publishing program. We also acknowledge the financial support of the **Government of Canada** through the **Canada Book Fund** and **Livres Canada Books**, and the **Government of Ontario** through the **Ontario Book Publishing Tax Credit**, and the **Ontario Media Development Corporation**.

J. Kirk Howard, President

Printed and bound in Canada.

Visit us at
Dundurn.com
Definingcanada.ca
@dundurnpress
Facebook.com/dundurnpress

Dundurn	Gazelle Book Services Limited	Dundurn
3 Church Street, Suite 500	White Cross Mills	2250 Military Road
Toronto, Ontario, Canada	High Town, Lancaster, England	Tonawanda, NY
M5E 1M2	LA1 4XS	U.S.A. 14150

Mick, Beauty, Angel
I love you more

Every time a bell rings, an angel gets his wings.
— *It's a Wonderful Life*

| FOREWORD |

It was December 23, 1993, when an editor yelled out, "Great story!" in the Toronto Sun building on King Street East in Toronto. A radio transmission had come through telling of a newborn that had been stolen from the maternity ward of a local hospital. Dressed as a nurse, a woman had entered Joseph Brant Memorial Hospital and fled with a mother's newborn. The human side of the story would not be realized until later, after the creation of a blockbuster headline. "It's a stolen Miracle," said one veteran in the newsroom. This was typical, as editors often write headlines while reporters run out the door to get to the scene. There is some truth to the old adage "if it bleeds, it leads." Of course, the people who work in news are not actually that crass — they have kids and feelings too. We care. But the story comes first. This was a heck of a story. A winner.

There's a Christmas wish list in newsrooms that editors and reporters working the holiday season know all too well. With short staffing and pages or time to fill, a big story during the holiday season is the present they all desire. They don't care if this gift is delivered from Santa or from a police radio.

At that time I was a 29-year-old, eight-year veteran of chasing stories. Most ended badly so I prepared myself for the worst. I had covered my share of just that. I hadn't seen many happy endings.

This baby's safety was on everybody's wish list — a gift not just for the media but for her family and everyone who followed the news of the child's loss. The impact of the baby's kidnapping was felt regionally and, ultimately, internationally. Even with the limited technology of the time, news travelled at lightning speed. This was before there were websites and blogs; I personally did not even have a cellphone. Security in hospitals was not as advanced as it is today, and there was no AMBER Alert in existence.

The details of this crime will follow and haunt a mother for a lifetime. The horror that was inflicted on her, her husband, and their children cannot be repaired, healed, or removed. For them it was not a headline or a great story, it was a nightmare. I remember thinking at the time that the story would make a great book, a story that people would be interested in long after the media had forgotten about it, long after the story was replaced with the latest headline grabber.

What this mom was subjected to is what is most compelling. Nothing can be taken for granted and nothing is for sure — even the safety of a newborn in the normally safe haven of a maternity ward.

How could one ever trust again?

For this baby's mother, there was a new reality. For Diana Walsh, writing the book *Empty Cradle* seems cathartic, her own form of personal therapy. It's reflective and real, honest and touching. This was an event she lived through, endured, and survived, but not without some bangs and bruises. While the media got its tremendous story and reporters went on to the next big scoop, the trauma for a family lingered. No simple trip to the store, or the seeing off of a child to school, would ever be quite the same.

Empty Cradle has everything from crime to pain and fear to sheer joy. But it's not a true-crime story in the usual sense. It's a mom's story.

Joe Warmington, *Toronto Sun*

| PREFACE |

If you were to ask five people about a specific event that they all experienced, each person would give you a completely different recollection. The truth is based on our personal perception, and this is the only reality we can engage with and the only one that really matters. This is my personal recollection of the days leading up to and surrounding the abduction of my five-day-old baby. The people close to me have assisted by filling in the blanks where my memory has failed.

For years I was unable to talk about the past. Privacy was my way of coping. I wasted a lot of energy building walls to protect myself, but walls eventually crumble, and unresolved traumas have a way of resurfacing. Writing became my voice. The more I wrote, the stronger I became; when I let go of all the secrecy and began to share my story, it helped me to heal.

Fifteen years after the event, I wrote *Empty Cradle*. This story is based on a true crime — the dates, times, and details were researched from media sources, court documents, and police records. Through this research I began to see my child's kidnapper as a person and not as a monster. With that said, I have taken liberties detailing the kidnapper's machinations and motivation, based on facts that I learned in the trial and thereafter. In the telling of this story, I have also taken similar liberties in outlining the actions of others, as well as the conversations that transpired.

Over 350 children are abducted in Canada each year, and the amount of pain and heartache felt when a single child goes missing is immeasurable. Imagine if it were your child: imagine what it would be like to go through every holiday, birthday, and milestone of your son or daughter's life, never seeing this part of you grow. Imagine going the rest of your life never knowing if your child was even alive.

When you pass a poster for a missing child, stop and take a good look. Remember the face, because no detail is insignificant; it could be that detail that makes the difference in identifying a lost or abducted child. You can contact Crime Stoppers and Child Find to discuss any information you may have on a missing child.

There are thousands of children that are not where they belong. They need to be reunited with their families. Watch for these missing children. Don't forget about them.

| PROLOGUE |

Stoney Creek, Ontario
December 23, 1993
11:30 P.M.

My bedroom is dark, lit only by a small beam of light, which is drifting in from the hallway. The house is quiet and still, now void of the commotion from earlier this evening. I lie motionless, fully clothed on top of the covers of my bed, staring at the ceiling. Although I have never been more tired in my life, my eyes are open as I pray:

> Please God ... help me.
> I'll do anything ... just keep her safe,

Please let me have her back.
Please God,
Please God.

Have you ever negotiated with God? Have you ever wanted something so bad that you would promise anything to get it? Have you ever begged for your life? I wish time would just pass, quickly so that the pain will lessen. Pass quickly so that I won't have to live with this uncertainty any longer. Let me wake up when I have the answers.

| CHAPTER 1 |

I am in the maternity ward of a small-town hospital, in the bed closest to the window. There are three other beds in the room. The curtain is drawn on my left side, separating me from the mother in the adjacent bed. I hear footsteps, someone entering the room — a common occurrence. A lumbering shape shuffles back and forth on the other side of the curtain, casting a shadow, but it seems insignificant.

This is the moment that will change my life. This is when the Shadow's plan comes to fruition. If she had come just ten minutes earlier, my family would have still been visiting me. I wouldn't have been alone, and my baby would never have been kidnapped.

But where does this story begin? To start here would be to forego so many significant details. My past has inextricably moulded me into the person I am today, and to appreciate the present I have to revisit it — as well as the past of another woman.

| Chapter 2 |

I come from a family of five children. These people are my best friends. Growing up, we were inseparable, and to some degree we remain that way today. The pecking order is as follows: my brother Chuck was the oldest, then Elaine, next Debbie, followed by me, and finally Maureen. We were one another's antagonists, but more often, confidantes and protectors. We would have gone to the wall for one another and often did. In this regard my family has never changed. Whenever I have needed them, my family have always been there for me, whether it was for something as serious as what we experienced in December of 1993 or something as simple as childhood pranks.

We grew up in Stoney Creek, a small town in southern Ontario, appropriately named for the pebble-lined creek that flows through its heart. At the time, Stoney Creek was the kind of town where no one locked their front door. In fact, in my early years I don't recall ever seeing a key to our house. I don't think there was one — we had nothing to fear. We had no reason to believe that any harm would befall us while we were in our homes, and it never occurred to us that a stranger might enter our homes during our absence.

Stoney Creek is known for several things, including the Battlefield Monument, the Stoney Creek Dairy, and the cornucopia of crops produced from the lush fruit belt. The Battlefield Monument commemorates the War of 1812 and the short but fierce battle that ensued on June 6, 1813, in Stoney Creek. We never thought much about this rich history; to us the battlefield was just the place where we went to watch fireworks on Victoria Day, piled under blankets to keep warm, and to picnic during the summer months, drinking in the intoxicating fresh air under the shade of the towering evergreen trees.

The Stoney Creek Dairy was and still is a source of employment for many students, and it remains a landmark. People come from miles away for a "topsy cone" or a "tin roof sundae." The ice cream is shipped across the country, and "Creekers" feel proud when, during their travels, they spot a sign in the window of some faraway place that reads WE CARRY STONEY CREEK ICE CREAM.

The neighbouring orchards were a place to have fun climbing a tree or picking fruit. Half of the excitement came from the fact that we didn't have permission for harvesting this bounty — in other words, we stole the fruit. When we climbed, we didn't worry about saving the trees or protecting the environment, we were just looking for the best way to build a fort or swing from the branches.

We relied on our bicycles to get around the single lane — often empty — streets. The bicycles were not ten-speeds — they were fixed-gear, often with a bell to ring and streamers flowing from the handlebars. We wouldn't think to ask our folks for rides to our friends' houses, and we knew to be home before the streetlights came on, often cutting through the fields and taking various shortcuts we had come to know and love to meet that deadline. When we went out we made sure we had a dime in our pocket for the pay phone. Later in life, as teenagers, if we weren't walking or riding our bikes, we also had thirty-five cents in our pockets for the bus.

When it was time for homework, everyone used the encyclopedia for research and sat together at the kitchen table with their freshly sharpened pencil crayons and ballpoint pens to handwrite their homework. Sometimes, the phone would be used to confer with a classmate. All the home phones were black. We didn't mind the time it took to dial those seven numbers — with one finger, around the rotary disc. We didn't know anything different. At that time, we didn't have to include the area code before the phone number, as there weren't enough homes to warrant such a thing.

It was unheard of to have two televisions, and the people who did have one usually just had a black and white set. Rabbit ears, which were fashioned from a bent coat hanger, could be seen sticking out of the back of our set to improve reception. The remote control hadn't been invented, and a man actually had to get up to change the channel. Kids didn't spend much time watching TV, because they spent most of their time outside with their friends or siblings.

Road hockey, ball, or hide and seek were good ways to bring the kids in the neighbourhood together, as was marbles in the dirt. Playing for "keepsies" was the only kind of gambling we did. If we won a bunch of Beauties from the neighbouring kids' marble collections, we hoped no one would make us give them back. Yet, if they won our Beauties, we hoped for the opposite.

Throughout our childhood, we all played on baseball teams and went to cheer one another on at the games in the community parks. Frequently, we would come home bruised and dirty but that was part of the fun; we were none the worse for wear.

The highlight of the week was my mom piling all five of us kids into the car and going to the library to bring home a bag of books. I loved walking into the library and beholding the walls and shelves lined with all those glorious publications. The book titles may have changed over the years, but the library still bears the distinct smell I remember from my childhood: the scent of thousands of works of art stored meticulously by category and author. The stories took us away from our daily lives and immersed us in a colourful world where anything was possible. I would bring as many books as I could carry to the counter and watch closely as the librarian stamped the little card with the return due date before inserting it into a pocket that had been glued to the inside of the book cover. Reading was a constant in our lives. To this day I never leave the house without a book in my possession.

On the weekends, we swam together in Lake Ontario. This was before there were signs and radio broadcasts warning of pollution. Someone would yell, "Last one in's a rotten egg," and we would race to jump into the water — we never knew the exact temperature, but it was cold enough to take our breath away. We lathered baby oil on one another's bodies, not sunscreen. The little sand flies that landed on our skin were trapped in the slippery globs and might have passed as a few extra freckles. We packed a lunch of PB&J sandwiches, and, if we were lucky, maybe some chocolate chip cookies to add to the mix. Squirrels would approach with caution to try and scavenge a few crumbs before the squawking seagulls beat them to it.

This was a time when siblings were best friends and played together day and night, a time when kids actually shared a bedroom and enjoyed it. The rooms didn't have matching duvets, curtains, and furniture; they housed a collection of odds and ends arranged to be cosy and practical, and were often in disarray, with unmade beds and belongings on the floor. Our parents had bigger fish to fry than caring about how tidy our room was.

When we were young, the four girls shared one room; we thought my brother was special because he had his own room. In our closet hung four matching dresses that Mom had sewn. Pink, blue, orange, and green sailor dresses hung side by side — except for the colour and size, they were identical in every way, and we wore them for church and special occasions.

The children all slept upstairs and my parents slept downstairs. Every night my mother would come upstairs to tuck us in. There was the predictable reading aloud, sometimes a little *Green Eggs and Ham* or a *Hop on Pop*, then kisses and lights out. Mom, true to form, could be heard as she walked away: "Sleep tight; don't let the bed bugs bite." Sometimes she would change it up and just say, "Sweet dreams."

When you have four girls rooming together and a brother in an adjoining room, shenanigans are inevitable. A typical night would include the old favourite, hide and seek, with hushed counting and tiptoed efforts to find the best hiding spot. The hiding spots were never too creative, as we only had about ten square feet to work with. Sooner or later, my mother would get fed up with all the giggling and little running feet and come marching back up to tell us to stop playing and go to sleep. Of course, by the time she got to the top of the stairs, we were all lying in bed like little angels. I can only imagine how frustrating this must have been for her after the strain of working multiple jobs and then returning home to the responsibility of her house and family. She was probably ready to strangle all five of us.

After several scoldings, she would sometimes say, "You kids better be quiet or I will send your father up." This was truly an idle threat, as my father was not the disciplinarian. After she left, you would sometimes hear one of us say, "Order in the court, order in the court. The monkey is about to speak." This was always followed by utter silence. It was hard not to talk, but no one wanted to be called a monkey. Then someone would laugh and everyone else would join in. Once again, a forbidden activity or game would begin. Someone on the bottom bunk bed would put their feet up and try to harass the person on the top bunk by bumping the mattress. On one such occasion, the top mattress came unhinged and came crashing down. We had to yell for my mother to come back upstairs and make a rescue, because the rest of us children weren't strong enough to lift the broken bed off of the troublemaker.

On another such night, one of my sisters — to this day I am sworn to secrecy as to which one — locked my brother in his room. He screamed bloody murder and banged on the door until his knuckles bruised. In his fury he promised he was going to "cream us" when he got out. The longer we left him in there, the madder he got. When we finally decided we should rescue him, we were too afraid to open the door, because we knew whoever he got his hands on first would be the target of his wrath. He finally escaped using a bent coat hanger, which he squeezed through a crack in the door to lift the hook out of the lock. When he freed himself, we all ran for cover, hoping not to be the one he caught first.

In the lazy days of summer, we participated in the day-camp activities at the Fruitland Community Centre. On the way home, we would cut through the surrounding orchards and partake of whatever fruit was in season. The fields were populated with hundreds of lush trees separated only by well-trodden dirt paths. As we walked along the paths and heard insects buzzing, birds chirping, leaves rustling, and the occasional piece of fruit dropping to the ground, there was an all too rare peacefulness. We helped ourselves to the crisp apples, the tart cherries, and the fuzzy, sweet peaches that, when plucked from their branches, left our skin tickling and itchy.

One day, while enjoying a handful of sun-kissed purple grapes, fresh from the vine, and concentrating on spitting out the tiny seeds, someone forcefully grabbed my arm. I looked up into the unshaven face of a very disgruntled farmer, who was sick and tired of all the kids trespassing through his fields and pinching his fruit. Although I knew he was angry, I could also tell from the glimmer in his eye and slant of his mouth that he was pleased at having caught me. I saw him as mean and nasty, not as a poor man just trying to make a living. "This is private property and you are trespassing. What is your name and where do you live?"

I looked around desperately only to find that my entourage had magically disappeared. The annoyed landowner repeated, louder this time, "What's your name?"

"... Diana ..."

Apparently that wasn't the answer he was looking for, and he was growing angrier by the second. "Your last name!"

Terrified, I looked down at my arm held firmly in his grip and quickly answered before his next question.

"Where do you live?"

Even though I was sure I was doing the wrong thing, I told him the house number and the street. It never occurred to me to be anything less than honest. As an adult, I look back on this day and wonder why I didn't make up some fictitious name and address or make a run for it. Surely my older sisters or brother would have been smart enough to think of that.

After I answered all of his questions and was finally released, I started running home with a sinking feeling in my stomach. I didn't stop until I met up with my siblings, who were sitting on the porch, waiting for me. They made me recount the entire conversation with the farmer. "You didn't tell him anything did you? You didn't give him your name right?"

It was bad enough that I had been stupid enough to get caught, but when they heard that I had answered the farmer's questions they were furious. We had an hour before my mom got home from work. I wasn't looking forward to that hour of scathing looks and recriminations. My mother was famous for saying that she trusted us and knew we would do the right thing. That was a heavy burden to carry, and none of us wanted to let her down. The worst thing that my mother could say was that she was disappointed in us. That was worse than any "lickin'" would ever be. Mom would sometimes tell us that we were "cruisin' for a bruisin'," but guilt hurt more than corporal punishment.

As we entered the house, the phone was ringing. My sister Elaine lunged for it, and with a perfect mommy voice she answered, "Hello. Yes it is. Oh my. They did? Well they will be punished I assure you and it won't happen again. Yes I understand. I'm very sorry and thank you for calling."

Everyone exhaled. Elaine had saved our bacon. My mom would never be the wiser. I was off the hook with my siblings, but I had trouble forgiving myself.

My mother's name is Marie Jeanne d'Arc, suitably named for the warrior Joan of Arc, and known to her friends as Joan. With an unwavering sense of humour, she worked hard to provide for her family, and she joined in all of our activities, supporting us unconditionally in everything we did. It is because of her that five young children made the choices they did and stayed on the straight and narrow.

When I married, my mom walked me down the aisle and I went from her arm to a future with my husband. When she married, for the second time, I walked her down the aisle and she went from my arm over to her future, with the man of her dreams. It wasn't traditional but it was fitting. My father did not show up for my wedding — or for my life, in many ways. However unavailable my father was, my mother made up for it with her wisdom, warmth, and understanding. She was my touchstone of stability and not only a mother to me growing up but also a father, as well as a friend.

| Chapter 3 |

My father was an alcoholic, which explains his absence both physically and emotionally. It also helps to explain a number of things about my family. Because of our feelings of shame, we felt the need to hide the truth of my father's addiction, and like him, we became very private individuals, masters at subterfuge.

We didn't know how commonplace substance abuse was. Had we known, we probably wouldn't have felt as isolated, but we didn't know and we never talked about it. My siblings and I had an exclusive club with a membership of five. My father called us "a bunch of reprobates." I grew up thinking this was a term of endearment.

There are many things that happen in an alcoholic home that defy reason. People struggling with addiction do some crazy things. On one occasion, my mother found one of my father's hidden bottles and promptly began to pour it down the kitchen drain. Upon discovering that his secret stash had been depleted, my father figured it was only fair to throw out the food in the house. Once this cockamamie decision was made, my father opened up the cupboards and looked in the fridge, grabbed whatever was in his reach, and began throwing groceries out the front door. Apparently the old adage "waste not want not" did not apply on this day.

Much to my horror, the paper boy was coming down the road to deliver the evening paper. This was a boy on whom I secretly had a crush. He was your stereotypical tall, dark, and handsome guy, with beautiful brooding eyes and more of a strut than a walk. He wore his T-shirt loose and his jeans tight. His white runners were appropriately scuffed to look dirty, and his hair, although long, was clean and styled to look like it hadn't been. As a barrage of food flew out the door and onto the front lawn, he kept on walking and didn't stop to make his delivery. Cereal escaping from the box, peanut butter, a couple of apples, cans of soup, and what was left of a loaf of bread all took on wings. My sister and I later laughed over the idea that the paper boy was probably afraid of getting beaned in the head with a flying roast.

Over the years, I discovered that there are many places to hide contraband. After a sleepless night, I told my sister I was like the princess and the pea, having discovered a bottle of vodka from beneath my mattress. I would find bottles in the most unlikely places — whether in drawers, a box of cereal, a winter boot, or the record player, there was no telling when one would turn up. My personal favourite, and one that made the most sense to me, was in the toilet tank. The alcohol well-hidden … but also well-chilled.

Whenever I came upon a hidden stash, I removed it. I took pleasure in messing with my father's head. When I imagined him returning to retrieve one of his bottles, I pictured the disappointment and confusion on his face as he came up empty-handed — had he already drank it, mixed up his hiding spots, or had someone found it? It wasn't like he could ask anyone. Perhaps he scratched his head as he walked away perplexed and thirsty.

He had tried to perfect this art of keeping his hidden bottles cold. On a blustery winter day, he slipped one into a wheel well of the car, resting it on top of the tire. He hadn't anticipated that if it snowed or rained the glass container would freeze to the rubber. Now he was presented with the serious problem of removing it without, God forbid, breaking it and losing some of its precious contents. My father thought that if he peed on the Mickey of gin he would be able to melt the ice enough to pry the bottle free. He took such care in hiding the evidence of his drinking and yet he had no qualms about openly urinating in the driveway to remove it. My dog, Ruff, watching this peculiar behaviour, followed his lead and right on cue lifted his leg and followed suit. It was just about this time that a familiar figure with a satchel full of newspapers looped over his shoulder was coming around the corner.

My father was tall, dark, and handsome, with brown eyes and wavy hair that he always kept well-groomed. When his hair started to turn grey at the sides, he darkened it with men's hair dye. His nose was cockeyed, veering slightly to the left — the result of a less than graceful exit from his car. He was always clean-shaven, and when I was little, I liked to watch him in the bathroom mirror as he dipped his shaving brush into hot water and then swirled it in leftover bars of soap he had in a little dish. As he smeared the lather on his face and dragged the straight-edge razor across his whiskers, he would smile and say, "What are *you* lookin' at?" I would wince on the occasions when, with shaking hands, he would nick himself with the blade and use a styptic pencil to quell the bleeding.

Although there must have been times when my father wore casual clothes, in my memories of him he is always attired in dress pants with matching shirt and tie. When I was in grade eight, he once came in my room wearing dark brown slacks and a white dress shirt, carrying two neck ties. I was listening to my transistor radio with my two girlfriends Colleen and Susan. Music was our life. Dad held the two ties up to his shirt and asked us, "Which one?"

Both my friends pointed to the solid light-brown tie in his left hand. I pointed to the tie that was striped gold, orange, and brown in his right hand. He stuck the plain brown tie in his pocket and began to wrap the striped tie around his neck. I was embarrassingly happy when he walked away whistling. As he exited the room, my friends said they still thought the brown tie was better.

He just looked over his shoulder and winked at me.

When my father was drinking, he turned from Dr. Jekyll into Mr. Hyde. He changed from a charming, handsome, witty man into an unattractive, belligerent — and often vulgar — sloppy drunk. His behaviour was a constant embarrassment to me. One night, as a child, I invited a friend of mine to sleep over. At the time my room was adjacent to that of my parents. As we were lying in bed, I heard the beginnings of an altercation between Mom and Dad. I started to breathe very heavily, partly because my heart was racing, but mostly because I was trying to make noise that would block out the sound of their arguing. As the situation escalated, so did the volume. The old furnace blew more than heat through the vent connecting the two rooms. I decided to add a loud snoring sound to my heavy breathing to further cover up the angry voices. I kept up this insane breathing, snorting, and coughing nonsense until I thought my friend had drifted off to sleep. I then lay quietly looking up at the ceiling, waiting for the battle to end. I awoke the next morning to my friend's eyes on me and her comment: "I heard them last night."

I never acknowledged her words. I never invited her to stay over again. It would be years before I invited a friend to sleep over again; I was not only humiliated because "she knew" but also because she likely thought I suffered from what we would now call sleep apnoea. Much later in life, I discovered that my friend's father also abused alcohol and, according to the rumour mill, his wife.

Although my father brought many challenges into my life, it would be wrong not to acknowledge how my life was also enriched by him. His sense of humour provided us with many laughs over the years, and his inconsistency, although irresponsible, was also something that drew my family together, particularly now as we look back from a distance.

Because of my father's unpredictability, I was taking a chance when I brought friends home unexpectedly — I never knew if I was coming home to the charming, handsome man or the sloppy drunk passed out on the floor. It was easier for me to plan around his absences. Very often, he disappeared for days on end. I never asked where he was during these stretches of blessed peace and quiet. I expect no one knew the answer. He was just gone.

Five children were delighted when he would return from one of his mysterious absences with a stray dog in tow. Heaven only knows where these dogs came from, but they all had some strange feature that made them a little less than perfect and a little more than loveable. Perhaps he saw a bit of himself in these lost and imperfect animals that just wanted to be loved. Over the years, we were the owners of a bizarre canine menagerie: A three-legged mutt that walked just fine, a dog with one blue eye and one brown, an incontinent spaniel, a jet-black dachshund that liked to play hockey with his nose, and a bulldog that drooled all over the house. Then there was the dog with the curly tail, and the one that appeared to be in constant heat, no matter what the season — we always seemed to be pushing it off someone or something.

Everyone's favourite was the collie/shepherd cross, the aforementioned and affectionately named Ruff, and like my father, Ruff would disappear for days on end. We would let him out in the yard, and when we called him to come back in, he would be gone. Just when we would give up hope of ever seeing our beloved dog again, he would show up on our doorstep with his tail wagging. Even today, Ruff is talked about with reverence. We also had a number of cats, fish, turtles, hamsters, and rabbits — this animal farm of pets provided a lot of comfort and love for five young children.

My father had a way of letting me know that he was aware of any transgression that I might have committed. He did it very subtly and without pointing a finger. On one Devil's Night, I was planning a rendezvous with my friend to soap some windows, so I searched for a new bar of soap in the house. I opened the bathroom drawer to find that it was crammed with clips, elastics, hair brushes, and makeup for a house of five women, but no soap. A metal nail file caught my eye, and I used it to saw the bathroom bar of white "Ivory" soap in half. I took my jagged, edged chunk of soap and snuck out to torment the neighbours, leaving the other half behind on the side of the sink. When I returned home from my debauchery, I wanted to escape to my bedroom as fast as possible so my family wouldn't notice the guilt radiating from me. I nonchalantly said good night to my parents and made my way up to my bedroom, where I was greeted with a message soaped across my dresser mirror in bold letters: HA HA, THE JOKE'S ON YOU. I knew, without question, my father was on to me, and this was just the type of thing that he would do to let me know.

Another example that comes to mind is when, as a teenager, I knocked the mirror off the side of the car while backing it out of the garage. I carefully put the mirror back in place, leaving it balancing very precariously on what was left of the base. The next morning, my father walked in to the house whistling, with the car mirror in his hand, and winked at me as he spoke to my mother: "The damnedest thing, as I was backing out of the driveway look what fell off."

My father whistled constantly. He also had a beautiful voice that he never wasted during sober moments; he preferred to belt out an old tune after "having a few." Sometimes a song on the radio reminds me of him, and I will smile as some pleasant memory creeps back into consciousness from long ago. Sometimes other visions creep back.

| CHAPTER 4 |

My father died at a young age. He abused his body for years, until it finally gave out on him in December 1991.

He was living alone around the time of his death, and had been since his separation from my mother years before. One week, during the Christmas holiday season, I was unable to reach him by phone. I shared with my husband that I had a bad feeling that something was wrong, then decided to drive over to my father's downtown apartment; on the seat beside me was the Christmas present I had wrapped for him — a framed photograph of his five children.

There was no answer when I pushed the buzzer for his apartment, so I waited for the next person to enter the building and followed closely behind her. The woman who entered before me looked over her shoulder as I hurried behind her down the hall and into the elevator, where I pushed the button to begin my ascent to the fifth floor. The elevator groaned and squeaked, jolting into action. As the elevator rose, a terrible stench began to penetrate the confined space. I looked accusingly at the person who was sharing my ride, and she looked suspiciously at me.

We exited the elevator together on the fifth floor. She went in one direction and I went the other, taking the few short steps to the door of my father's apartment. I put my ear to the door and listened — I wanted to snoop before I knocked, because knowing my father, he would pretend he wasn't there. If I listened beforehand, some telltale noise might give him away.

There were muffled sounds of the television set and his pet bird squawking, but nothing else.

After looking around to make sure I was alone, I got down on my knees and looked in the mail slot. Sometimes crazy begets crazy. I could only make out some flickering lights — still no Dad. I got up and knocked on the door. No answer. I went back down to the mail slot and called in to him: "Dad, are you in there...? It's me." When there was no response, I tried another tactic. "I am leaving something outside the door for you."

I scrunched the wrapping paper on the Christmas gift as loudly as possible before leaving it leaning against the door, then stomped in an exaggerated fashion down the hall toward the elevator and ducked into the alcove of another apartment door. I stood very quietly and waited, but he didn't open his door.

Waiting was obviously getting me nowhere, so I went back down to the lobby and knocked on the door marked SUPERINTENDENT. I was greeted by a pasty-white face that had not seen much sun over the last decade and was topped by a head of greying hair that had seen a bottle or two of Grecian Formula. He was a rotund fellow in a white undershirt and black polyester pants, which badly needed a belt, and he was looking at me curiously. I introduced myself and asked if he would let me into my father's apartment. He agreed so readily that I wondered if it was a common request. He then went back into his apartment and came out with a noisy ring of keys, fumbling around with them in one hand and pulling up his baggy trousers with the other as we walked to the elevator.

Instead of talking, we just watched the numbers change as the elevator made its rickety ascent up several floors and finally jolted to a stop. The door creaked open to reveal that we had stopped a couple of inches below the floor, but there was no reaction from my silent ally, so apparently this was to be expected in the old building. We stepped up to exit the elevator, and as we were walking down the grey, stained carpeted hallway to my father's door, my nostrils were again assaulted with the fetor of rotten garbage. The foul odour elicited no response from the superintendant.

After one last unanswered knock on the door, the superintendent turned the key. The doorknob twisted for me, but the door wouldn't budge more than a crack. Through the slight opening I yelled, "Dad it's me, I just want to make sure that you're all right, let me in." I had visions of him barricading the doorway — it was just the kind of irrational behaviour I had come to expect from my father, but the only response was that of the squawking bird. It sounded like it was being strangled in the jaws of a very hungry cat. "Dad! Open the door!"

I threw my weight against the entrance and was rewarded with a slight movement of the door and a sore shoulder. Through the few inches the door had opened, I could see a scooter parked on the opposite side, acting as a barricade. As the superintendent watched with fascination, I heaved myself once more against the door and created an opening large enough for me to squeeze through. Without looking back, I entered the apartment. The repugnant smell grew stronger.

The only illumination in the dark room was the flickering light of the television. It cast strange, distorted shadows on the walls and floor. The caged bird was in hysterics, flying around so chaotically that feathers and bird litter were exploding between the bars and spiralling onto the floor.

When I stepped farther in to the room, I saw my father sitting on the couch, staring straight ahead at the television, with his arm lazily draped over the back of the sofa. He did not turn his head to look at me. My eyes travelled to the coffee table in front of him, where there was a glass that was half full. I realized that his body was there, but the soul of William Alfred Martin Elson, my father, was no longer present.

He must have been dead for several days. With no ventilation in the small, warm apartment, my father's body was in the advanced stages of decomposition.

I couldn't help it.... I took a step closer. In morbid fascination, I looked at his feet. Although they were grotesquely puffy, it occurred to me that they looked a lot like mine. They were in a puddle of some dark body fluids, which were still escaping from various orifices and had spread to cover most of the floor. I looked down to see if I was standing in the sea of darkness and found that I had stopped just inches short of it.

Mercifully, the dimness made it difficult for me to see and I made no attempt to turn on the lights. My eyes made a slow ascent up his distorted body. I saw his bloated remains in shades of purple and black. His only clothing, a pair of tighty-whiteys that were not so white. His belly was so distended it looked like it might explode at any moment — I could hear it gurgling and rumbling. His face was contorted into a mask, with eyes the size of golf balls and a protruding black tongue, that did not resemble my father in any way.... But those feet ... They were definitely his feet. With utter sadness and a sense of unreality, my own feet started taking slow steps backwards. Past the coffee table, past the sea of darkness, past the television that was still flickering with some unknown program, the people cheering and clapping, past the hysterical bird and the now-insignificant mess it had made on the floor, past the scooter, until I reached the door, with the knowledge that dark rooms would forever thereafter instill in me a tremor of fear. I squeezed myself through the narrow opening, back out into the hall, where the bright lights were momentarily blinding.

The superintendent was staring at me.

"He's dead," I said quite matter-of-factly.

The poor fellow looked at me like I had gone mad. "Are you sure?"

"Positive."

I guess he had to see for himself, because he squeezed himself through the opening, not an easy task for the portly man. After what seemed like mere seconds, he rushed back out. With eyes watering and a hand covering his mouth, he choked and gagged. I don't know why this struck me as funny. In my head I was saying, *Do you believe me now?* Between coughs, he croaked out a few words: "Oh my dear ... I'm so sorry...."

"Do you have a phone I could use?"

The superintendent didn't immediately answer me. He watched me for a few seconds, then nodded his head and, without a sound, turned and started walking away. I followed him back to the elevator and we made our way back down. The sounds I had found so distracting on the way up to my father's apartment were now not even registering in my mind.

Like the chronic coke users I had seen in the movies, I kept rubbing my face. Although we were far removed from my father's apartment, the smell still burned my nose and throat. I wondered how in the world people worked in homicide.

The superintendent showed me into a small office that was so crammed with junk I had to walk sideways to reach the dirty beige phone on the wall. Without hesitation, I called the person I knew I could always count on: my husband. Without preamble, I began. "Well he's here.... But he's dead."

I went on to tell him what had happened and asked him to come and help me. I asked him not to call anyone yet — I didn't know what I was going to say to them. My husband knew whom I referred to when I said "them." It was not news that I was looking forward to sharing. My husband assured me that he would come right away, and after hanging up the phone, he called my brother. He knew what I needed before I did.

My fingers next dialled 911.

"Emergency response can I help you?"

"Hello, I've just come to visit my father and found him dead. I'm not sure what to do...."

"Are you sure he is dead?'

This question was predictable and I provided the answer. "Positive."

"Can you tell me the address of where you are?"

The address momentarily escaped me. I slowly opened the drawers in the filing cabinet of my mind, pulled out the correct folder, and finally found the appropriate paper with the information I was looking for. I remembered the street, which I recited, "Jackson Street …," but for the life of me, I couldn't remember the number of the building. I pulled an address book out of my purse, and when the inquiry was made for a second time, I was ready with the correct response. After answering all of the questions that were asked of me, I made my way back up to the fifth floor. This time I took the stairs and avoided the elevator. By the time I got back to the apartment, the paramedics had already arrived, as had the police and the fire department. *Wow, such a response and at lightning speed. Everyone and their brother is here*, I thought. And just then, I looked up to see mine come running down the hall toward me. I travelled back in time and remembered my father singing an old Al Jolson song, "Sonny Boy," to my brother. It has poignant lyrics that express beautifully the love a father feels for a son.

I don't remember what was said between us. I suppose we didn't need words so much as we needed each other. Standing together in the hallway, we answered a police officer's questions.

"How old was your father?"

"I can't remember. His birthday was in November ... just a few weeks ago." Looking up at my brother, I watched him give the correct answer.

"He was fifty-nine."

"Was your father ill? Did he have any health issues?"

"Well ... he abused alcohol for many years," I said. *Am I betraying him with my response?* This was not something I had ever said to a friend, let alone a stranger.

"How long has it been since you last spoke to him?"

I remembered his belligerent drunken rants and, conversely, his quiet sombre periods of introversion, when he spoke to no one. I couldn't tell them, "I've never really had a conversation with my father — not about anything of consequence," so instead I said, "He was a very good looking man."

After my inappropriate response, the police officer looked over to my brother. The officer seemed so young. *Are police much younger these days?* My brother didn't add anything to my comment. He walked over to the apartment door and put his hand on the doorknob. I wish I could have said, "Don't do it. Don't go in there," but I said nothing. After some pondering, his hand dropped to his side and his chin down to his chest. He stepped away from the door and wisely chose not to enter the apartment.

By then the use of the elevator was restricted, so my husband appeared from the stairwell door and joined us. I welcomed the open arms that encircled me and the strength that they offered. I now had the two most important men in my life to support me, men whose love and respect I could always count on. I was not alone. I started to head toward the stairs. There was nothing more we could do. It was time to leave the building and my father.

The paramedics could be heard behind me, telling my brother and my husband that what I had seen in the room might be difficult to deal with and it might be a good idea for me to "talk to someone." I never did.

After much resistance from my two heroes, who both wanted to drive me home, we all got back in our own vehicles and drove separately. I had time to grieve in private as we made our way back to my brother's house. My tears were a secret, like everything else.

Before entering my brother's home, I dropped my outer layers of clothing at the doorway, believing they would carry that rotten stench forever. Although the clothes were left outside, I could still smell death. I felt like I would never be clean again.

Someone offered me a drink from the liquor cabinet, but I shook my head, *no*. I didn't want anything or anyone to loosen my resolve. I was determined to hold myself together. As I drank several glasses of water in quick succession, I wondered what my father's last thoughts were for those fleeting moments, after his heart gave out and before his mind did. I imagine, knowing my father, he thought his glass was half empty and only wished he'd had the time to finish it.

My sister-in-law, Beverly, wrapped me in a blanket, under which I continued to shiver. I chalked the chills up to the ice water, but even after a cup of coffee, my body continued to shake. We sat at the island in the kitchen, and my brother began to make the phone calls to my sisters. I met his eyes while he dialled and continued to hold them while he spoke. "I'm afraid I have some upsetting news...."

I felt my eyes once again start to fill, felt the blotches appearing on my face. My nose, already stuffy from my recent overflow of tears, was now completely plugged. I had to breathe through my mouth as I listened to my brother's calls.

I thought this would be the worst day of my life.

| CHAPTER 5 |

1943

In Muskegon, Michigan, the Shadow of a child is curled up in her bed, humming. At three years old, going on four, she is a toddler who is transforming into a little girl without anyone even noticing. The auburn curls that fall across her pillow have never been decorated with a bow. She is wearing pyjama bottoms and a stained undershirt. On her feet she wears two different socks. There are no fancy dresses hanging in her closet. On the floor, beside her bed, a glass lies on its side, but it goes unnoticed beneath a pile of clothes. She has exactly two playthings: a dinky toy car and her dolly with matted hair and eyes that shut when she lays her down. She is talking quietly to Dolly as she covers her with the only blanket on the bed.

"Mommy's tired. You be a good little girl and go to bed and I don't want to hear a sound out of you."

She shares a room with her three older siblings, and as she rolls over, she puts her thumb in her mouth, but discreetly so that they won't see her do it. She doesn't want them to have any ammunition to tease her with tomorrow. Her father is an alcoholic. So is her mother. She has no touchstone of stability. She can hear her parents' fury raging down the hall.

"All you care about is going to the hotel to meet your drinking buddies."

"All YOU care about is finding ways to drive me crazy. Maybe if you would get off my back, I would stay home once in a while."

"I can't stand to look at you."

"God damn it, you won't have to look at me any longer."

There are sounds of crashing furniture and a door slamming.

"You come back here, don't you walk out on me."

A glass shatters, and the child resumes her humming.

Soon after, the child is seized from her home and put up for adoption. When she leaves her home, she doesn't realize it is for good. When she says goodbye to her family, she doesn't understand it is forever. In her new home, when she discreetly puts her thumb in her mouth, she wishes her siblings were there to tease her.

| CHAPTER 6 |

I met my husband, Glenn, when I attended Orchard Park High School at the age of sixteen. It was one of two high schools at the time in Stoney Creek. We sat beside each other in art and history classes. We talked at great length when we should have been listening. The discussions continued out of class, as did the longing. We started to spend time together away from school, and our status gradually changed to boyfriend and girlfriend. We were "going around" together.

This was about the time that my mother started using all of the clichéd adages on me: "Choose your friends wisely because you are judged by the company you keep," "Never leave your drink unattended when you are away from home," "Stay away from people who are pushing drugs." The most predictable, and the one that gave my siblings and me much amusement over the years, was, "kissing leads to other things."

The apple doesn't fall far from the tree. The other day I heard myself say to my daughter, "Kissing leads to other things." It was out of my mouth before I knew what I was saying. When I saw her smirk, I had to grin myself. I was now the mother counselling her daughter. My mother used to say to me that she remembered what it was like to be my age, and I never believed her, but I still made the same claim to my daughter, knowing full well it would fall on deaf ears.

I remember a conversation I had with my mother later in life, in which she told me that every generation in their turn thinks they are the first ones to discover music, alcohol, drugs, and sex, but as much as things change, they remain the same. Turns out, Mom was right.

During high school, Glenn and I had dreams of who we wanted to be and what we wanted to do. Our idea of how the world worked was gleaned from our small-town upbringing and immediate circle of family and friends. As teenagers, we didn't know how limited our experiences were, or that we weren't as smart as we thought we were. We were incapable of thinking years ahead, and our thoughts seldom travelled more than a week in advance. We easily judged those older than us, because we knew everything, although we didn't even have access to the kind of global community that we would see just a decade later, with the widespread use of computers and the Internet. Facebook, Twitter, and Blackberries did not yet exist, and the global news was not broadcasted, minute by minute, to almost every home in the developed world.

After high school we both continued our studies at Mohawk College in Hamilton, although in the seventies, post-secondary education was the exception not the expectation. I enrolled in recreation and leisure studies, and Glenn studied industrial engineering. This was back when the Mohawk's Arnold Centre, the student pub, was located outside the school walls in a cave-like brown-brick structure and could only house a couple dozen students. The "Arny" has since moved indoors to the cafeteria area, where it accommodates hundreds. The recreation students were among the Arny's best clients, as they downed copious amounts of draught beer and played their favourite drinking games. Maybe this is why the old Arnold Centre structure now houses the recreation department faculty and staff.

Like most young people, we thought we were infallible. We did crazy, careless things in college, before we had to worry about maintaining families of our own — children, bills, our health, and consequences in general. It was our time to laugh loud and party hard. We were adventurous, made mistakes and learned lessons. It never occurred to us that it was dangerous to drive fast. We never thought about the hazards of driving when overtired. We never realized just how damaging drinking and driving was. What's more, these thoughtless habits were just reinforced when police officers would pull over a carload of reckless teenagers and then send them on their way with only a cursory warning.

One evening some acquaintances of mine were returning from a late night out, when they rolled up to the Burlington lift bridge on the edge of town, which was rising to allow a vessel to pass underneath. Since this can take a relatively long time, the driver put the car in park as they waited for the bridge to return to the ground. As they listened to the classic 70s hit, "Paradise by the Dashboard Light," the laughter and singing slowly faded, and everyone in the car fell asleep, including the driver.

Long after the bridge had returned to the ground and the other cars waiting to cross had passed and gone on their merry way, the group of teenagers continued to sleep with the car running. The rest was not meant to continue, however, as a passing officer pulled up behind them, got out of his car, and rapped his flashlight on their window. After the driver recovered from being so rudely awakened, he rolled down the window.

"Excuse me. Care to tell me what you're doing?" the officer asked.

"… Oh, hello officer. I must have fallen asleep."

"Well ... wake up and you kids get yourself home. You're blocking the road."

While it may be surprising to people of today, used to strict rules and regulations, that is the end of the story — and that type of interaction wasn't uncommon. Another friend told me of a similar story, where she was pulled over by a police officer for driving too slow.

"Miss, do you realize how slow you are driving?"

"I'm sorry officer. I've had a lot to drink, so I was just taking my time."

"Well would you please speed up. You're holding up traffic."

These things happened all the time, and we laugh as we recount the stories. We all have one, and we continue to wonder why the laws were so lackadaisical and we were so careless.

During those years, we lost many close friends, and among those taken from us were three young men that we grew up with. Jimmy lost his life in the wee hours of the morning after driving too fast along a single-lane highway. Steve's car went off the side of the escarpment. Three people were in the car that night as it careened around a corner and over the Dundas hill. Steve lost his life. He would not live to know the consequences of this night on the town. He would never know that his friend in the passenger seat did not survive the crash. He also wouldn't know that Rob, crammed in the back of the sports car, sustained lifelong injuries and would forever carry the memory of two lost friends — a burden that only an extreme trauma survivor can imagine or understand.

Jimmy and Steve were joined by Mark, Colleen, and many others, as we learned how compassionate the Browns could be at their family-run funeral home.

It became evident to many of us — although surprisingly not all — that reckless behaviour, excessive drinking, and drug use correlated directly with teenage mortality.

Unprotected sexual relations were also common and of no concern. The only thing that was thought to be dangerous was an unexpected pregnancy. AIDS and other sexually transmitted diseases were not yet part of our vocabulary or our experience, so the appropriate precautions were not readily taken by the masses. The value of protection or abstinence only became evident after many of our generation had already been exposed to the dangers of casual sex.

When you think of the opportunities for disaster, it's a wonder that more of us didn't suffer tragedy or lose our lives at a young age. In retrospect, the saying "There, but for the grace of God, go I" seems more accurate every day.

| CHAPTER 7 |

The Shadow of a girl has had a troubled childhood. Although her adoptive parents are loving and supportive, they cannot fill the gap left by her missing siblings and biological parents. Her parents often find her sitting on the floor, crying. Her repeated wish upon a star goes unanswered — her constant requests for her brothers are a waste of time. She is not reunited with them and eventually stops asking.

Her adolescence is equally turbulent, and happiness is always slightly beyond her grasp. The adoptive parents bring her to speak to a psychologist, but the young girl is non-communicative.

Varieties of socially unacceptable behaviours give her an immediate high but do not bring lasting fulfillment. She sneaks the occasional cigarette — as she blows the smoke out of her bedroom window, she feels a little nauseous and a lot guilty. Searching for thrills as a way to lift her spirits becomes second nature. At the age of fifteen, she steals a car and tries to drive over the border to Canada. The brief feeling of power and freedom she feels ends when she is apprehended and returned to her adoptive parents. She is loved but never understood. She does not want to hurt her parents, but she can't help herself — her regret is crushing. In high school she meets someone special and falls in love. He is steadfast and true. She finds satisfaction in her relationship, and the risks that were once a part of her daily life are not so appealing anymore.

At sixteen years of age, she has become a bride — married to a twenty-one-year-old man. She is a teenager who has been thrust into the role of a wife. This is her chance to redeem herself. She will become a good wife and mother.

She is not old enough to legally drive. She is not old enough to vote or legally drink, but she is a married woman. As a married woman, she returns to classes in the fall and completes high school in the United States of America. In "the land of opportunity," she has dreams of who she wants to be and what she wants to do. She puts her troubled past behind her and goes on to a community college, where she completes a practical nursing course. With an altruistic attitude, she decides she will spend the rest of her life as a health care professional. It looks as if she faces a bright future.

| CHAPTER 8 |

After many years of dating, I finally persuaded my boyfriend to say I do, and we did. I married my high-school sweetheart in November 1985. We had our ten siblings standing beside us, in their matching finery, as we said our vows in St. Francis Xavier Church on Highway 8 in Stoney Creek. We promised to love each other "till death do us part." With my fingers crossed, I also promised to "love honour and obey." I was okay with the love and honour part, but I had a little problem with the "obey" component — I believe they have since taken that traditional imperative out of wedding vows.

Within a few months of marriage, my clothing started to get tight around the middle. I joined a Weight Watchers class offered during lunch hours at my place of employment, kept track of my food intake, and remained active, yet my weight kept increasing.

When I shared this with one of the girls at work, she asked if I could possibly be pregnant, and the idea took me by surprise — I hadn't kept track of my monthly schedule. My husband and I had hoped to have a family right away but didn't expect it would happen so quickly, so I went to my doctor to investigate my co-worker's suggestion. After some small talk, the doctor asked if I had any signs or symptoms of pregnancy. "I don't know ... what are the symptoms?" I replied.

"Have you had any headaches or have you been constipated?"

I answered yes to both of the questions.

"Have you had to urinate more than usual?"

Yes again.

"Any lower back pain?"

As a matter of fact ...

"Have you had any unusual aversions to foods or smells?"

I couldn't stand the smell of meat and hadn't eaten it for weeks. I also couldn't stand the smell of beer, which was unusual for me.

"Have you been tired?"

I could fall asleep sitting at my desk.

The doctor smiled. "Well, sounds like you're expecting."

The blood test confirmed her prediction, and my first child was due on our first anniversary.

When you are a pregnant woman of five-foot-one, your child doesn't have much room to grow up or down. My girth increased rapidly and profoundly. By the time I was four months pregnant, I had replaced all of my regular clothing with a maternity wardrobe. I felt as wide as I was tall, and I looked like one of those roly-poly dolls that keeps bouncing back up after you push it down.

After having my unusually large measurements taken at a routine checkup, the doctor predicted I would have twins and arranged an ultrasound to confirm her suspicions. At fifteen weeks the ultra sound showed one healthy baby, which looked like a curled up shrimp with a tiny, pulsing chest. As the technician completed her examination, she explained that this pulsing was the heartbeat, and she continued to point out different parts of the body while I strained to see the various extremities and features. The sex of the baby was not revealed, and I didn't reveal my preference to anyone. Secretly — and guiltily — I hoped for a baby girl.

My pregnancy moved along without any complications. I felt great. It was a wonder to me, this experience of a child growing inside of me. It was one of the only times in my life that I would welcome the growing size of my waistline with enthusiasm and a lack of self-consciousness. I chose to have dessert without hesitation, and how about a little bit of butter on those vegetables!

The first time I felt movement from the baby, I was cutting the lawn and stopped dead in my tracks. The motor sputtered to a stop as I removed my hands from the mower and put them on my abdomen. Outwardly, I could feel nothing, so I couldn't share the exciting news with anyone, but inwardly the fluttering continued like butterfly wings and I was ecstatic. I walked around for weeks with a subtle smile on my face, marvelling at the blossoming of this bud and the feelings of motherhood that were also growing within me.

Months later I relished the fact that other people could feel the baby move with the touch of a hand or simply watch the stripes of my maternity shirt ripple as the baby struggled to get comfortable. I rested my guitar on my abdomen, and as I strung the chords to "Blowin' in the Wind" and "Hush Little Baby," I sang without abandon.

For nine months I was in awe. I couldn't wait for the big day.

| CHAPTER 9 |

My due date came and went, but the stork did not. I called one of my sisters, who had just had her third child. Between bites of red licorice, I lamented, "Nothing's happening and it's two weeks past my due date."

She responded, "Any day now, just hang in there. When the baby is ready it will come."

"My skin is stretched so far it's starting to crack. It's so itchy I could tear it apart." I looked down at my huge belly. "It's amazing that you grow all of this extra skin and then it just goes away after you have a baby."

She hesitated. "Yes, it is amazing."

It sounded to me like she was laughing, but I didn't know what was so funny.

I was ready. My overnight bag was packed — toiletries, reading material, a white cotton nightshirt to wear at the hospital, and a yellow jumpsuit (non-maternity) to wear home. I tried upping my activity to bring on labour, cutting the lawn whether it needed it or not. When I rode my bicycle, the neighbours got a kick out of watching me pedal around the block while trying to avoid hitting my protruding belly with my knees. In the end, the "old wives's tale" proved to be a myth: activity didn't bring on the baby any faster. I had no idea what to expect, but I knew it hadn't happened yet, and I figured I would recognize it when the time came.

As it turned out, that was two weeks after the expected due date, when I went into labour shortly after midnight. I had been right in that I would recognize the onset of labour when the time came, but I had underestimated the strength with which it would overtake me.

It seems everyone has a birth-related story to tell, and you can *bet* they are not about the chocolate and roses they received. I thought everyone was exaggerating with their yarns, that childbirth couldn't be as bad as they were making it out to be. After all, when I had my wisdom teeth out, the experience proved to be much easier than everyone had predicted. The same held true when I had my tonsils removed.

With this, my first child, Michael, I learned that labour is the perfect word to describe the experience of birthing a child. During the eighteen hours I was in labour with my son, I completely trashed my hospital room.

My uterine muscles were spiralling from top to bottom. As they contracted to push the baby down the birth canal, there was an earthquake in my body. Like tectonic plates, my bones shifted to make way for the baby. This cataclysm was unparalleled to anything I had ever experienced, and the staggering pain rendered me speechless. I centered every bit of effort on the contractions and wasted none on words. When my husband suggested playing cribbage to pass the time, I didn't even try to tell him why that was a bad idea.

With hopes of speeding up the blessed event, I paced the room. When the tidal wave of a contraction came over me, I would stop and lean over the bed. The blankets on the bed were my bullet to bite, and I squeezed handfuls of material with all my might. The white sheets within my grasp came untucked during the frenzy and now lay discarded on the floor beside a fallen pillow. The hanging beige curtain was tangled in the bed railing, and when the rollaway hospital cart got in my way, I shoved it across the room, where it bounced off of the wall, knocking a chair askew on the way. The small Kleenex box that started on the window sill was knocked to the floor and now crunched beneath my foot. My room looked like a war zone.

When one of the nurses entered, she looked around and said, "Maybe we should get you into bed."

As I was approaching the finish line, another mother was brought into the room. There were only two beds in the labour area of the small hospital, and she was quickly undressed and helped into the adjacent bed. The nurses made sure the curtain beside me was drawn, but it was a poor sound barrier for the shrieks coming from my new roommate.

A doctor entered the room close behind her and spoke to the attending nurse. "How far along is our first patient?"

"She's eight centimetres."

"This patient is nine, and has had other children — she'll probably go much quicker. Move her in to the delivery room."

There was only one delivery room, adjacent to where we waited, through a door mere inches away, and only one doctor. I looked imploringly at the nurse as she wheeled the gurney by me.

"Hold tight. You're next," she said with a smile.

I'm next ... wait a minute ... not fair... I'm not on deck, I'm up to bat. I'd been waiting for hours, and this expectant mother had just arrived. This was not the way that I imagined this day would be. In my fantasy everything went smoothly: I was propped up in bed, looking like Lady Diana, well-groomed in my crisp cotton nightshirt, not a hair out of place. I'd be serene as I easily gave birth to my child, and I'd look the same after the delivery. In the evening following the birth, I would feel great — light as a feather — back to my pre-pregnant weight. I would snack on a box of chocolate truffles as I passed the time reading my new novel.

Beyond the wall separating us, I could hear bloodcurdling screams. Reality was hot on my heels. I didn't know what exactly was going on behind that closed door, but it scared the hell out of me — by the look on Glenn's face, he was also concerned. One of the nurses came to check on me every few minutes. "Don't worry, you'll be fine. It won't be long now."

The doctor was right: the other child came first. I now heard the sound of a baby crying, signalling that it was my turn. The nurse handed over sterile hospital gown and blue paper slippers to Glenn. "Okay, Dad, put these on and follow us."

Once in the delivery room, the mystery of childbirth was revealed to me. It was the most intense upheaval imaginable, yet minutes later, at 5:02 p.m., I was sitting on a cloud holding my seven-pound baby boy, without a care in the world. Once I looked into the big blue eyes of my first-born child, I immediately forgot the previous eighteen hours of labour. Even now, I can remember the experience and my actions but not the searing pain. If you would have spoken to me minutes after he was born, I would have said, "That wasn't so bad." I held him close as I studied the white-blonde hair on his slightly squished head and every feature of his wrinkled little body. He looked like a mini octogenarian. I told him how I loved him to the sun and the moon and the stars and around the world and back again. I decided at that moment that I had wanted a baby boy all along — a beloved son. His siblings would have the big brother that I had growing up. There was no better way to start a family.

The happiest times are when babies come. My family came to visit, equipped with champagne and presents. I snapped pictures of them either holding the baby or sipping bubbly. At the end of each day, one of the nurses brought in a basin of warm water and fragrant soap. The nurse's sponge bath was followed by soothing cream, a sprinkle of baby powder, and some advice: "When your husband comes home at the end of the day, put on some fresh lipstick and no matter how tired you are, always greet him with a smile."

I left the hospital filled with wonder at the kindness of these nurses, who took such care in ensuring my comfort and well-being. I also left the hospital a self-proclaimed addict — I was a *photoholic.*

I took photographs of the nursery, which was freshly painted yellow to accommodate the arrival of either a baby boy or a baby girl. I took pictures of the baby paraphernalia: the receiving blankets under the change table, still creased from the way they had been folded in the department store; the well-intentioned cotton diapers and the colourful safety pins beside them — these would very quickly be replaced with disposable diapers with tape fastenings. Everything was snapshot worthy — feeding, changing, bathing, sleeping....

I had joined the ranks of those sappy parents who were hopelessly in love with their newborns.

I would hold my newborn until he fell asleep every night, begrudgingly putting him down to lie on colourful flannel sheets that smelled of fabric softener. Throughout the night I would creep back to the nursery and watch him sleep. Everything was a delight.

Any bad memories were long gone. I wanted another child.

| CHAPTER 10 |

One year later, when the smell of meat turned my stomach and I once again had no interest in beer, I knew my wish had come true. As in the past, the doctor took measurements and predicted twins. However, an ultrasound showed one healthy baby and a further blessing of no expected complications.

Again, the sex of the baby was not revealed, and again I didn't reveal my preference to anyone. Secretly and guiltily I hoped for another baby boy — a brother to keep Michael company. I didn't have the experience of growing up in a house full of boys, but Glenn did and I'd heard all the stories. Glenn's mother, Patricia, had six boys in a row before she had her daughter, Mary, and the neighbours put up a banner that read FINALLY A GIRL!

Six boys: that's a lot of testosterone, and a lot of groceries. Glenn's father, Patrick, would buy a side of beef to feed the family for the winter. His yearly hunting trips for moose also helped to stock the freezer. Patricia would make fresh bread every week and dozens of pies to accompany her nightly home-cooking. Witnessing dinner at their table was like watching a game of rugby, everyone reaching and pushing for the meat and potatoes, strategically guarding what was on their plates lest an older sibling claim his birthright and swipe something.

There were enough boys to put together an informal game of road hockey or basketball. When it came to organized sports, they walked to the little league park for baseball and the Stoney Creek Arena to play hockey, and they sometimes had to share equipment. Often they were on the same team, but if they had the misfortune to play on a different one, the second guy on the ice had to wear recently used, and likely damp, gloves or pads. On one occasion their mother mistakenly purchased football pads for the hockey season, but they still did the trick and were passed on down the ranks.

In the summer months, there were enough boys to create an incredible whirlpool as they ran in a circle around the edges of their above-ground pool, creating a current that was strong enough to sweep them off of their feet. They shared bedrooms and disagreements were often settled with fists, but the fights were quickly forgotten, and any inconveniences presented by having five brothers were outweighed by the fact that they always had one another's backs — whether it was in a game or in real life. There's something to be said for having a brother.

On September 1, as my son, Michael, was sleeping soundly, the first rumblings of labour began, again two weeks past my due date. I started watching the clock at 2:00 a.m. and noted that the tightenings in my abdomen were coming in about thirteen-minute intervals. A vague memory started to rear its ugly head. I felt excited yet scared, like I was slowly being carried up a roller coaster, waiting for the thrill of the downward ride. My eyes were glued to the glowing red numbers on the alarm clock in my dark bedroom. Lying beside my sleeping husband, I had a pencil in my hand and a piece of paper on the bedside table, and I started charting numbers down a page: 2:00, 2:15, 2:30, 2:45, 2:53, 3:01, 3:09, 3:16, 3:23 — I gave Glenn a nudge, "Seven minutes apart."

With a sleepy voice that showed no sign of concern or enthusiasm, Glenn responded, "Should we call Maureen?"

Remembering the eighteen hours of waiting for Michael, I thought we had lots of time before we would have to call my sister. "No, let's give it a little longer." I continued to watch the clock, 3:45, 3:50 … *3:50!* We had jumped to five minutes between contractions, and things were moving quickly.

At 4:00 a.m., while I was bent over with a contraction, Glenn called Maureen. "Hi Moe, it's time — can you come up to the house and stay with Michael?"

As the contractions started to let up, I called to him from down the hall, "Tell her not to hurry … tell her everything is fine and … tell her to drive carefully."

Maureen was eight months pregnant. She was expecting her first child, and she looked ready to deliver at any moment. I will never forget opening the door, in the wee hours of the morning, to see her smiling from ear to ear, wearing a flannel nightgown, and carrying her cream-coloured satin pillow under her arm. She apologized for her delay, adding that she'd had to stop for gas on the way up because her car was on empty. I would have enjoyed witnessing my eight-months-pregnant little sister, in her pyjamas, pumping gas before the morning sun had risen. We hugged each other as tightly as we could, with our two babies bulging between our love and laughter.

Glenn and I made our way out to the car, and I stopped once in the driveway as I buckled over and let a contraction run its course. When it passed I looked over my shoulder to see Maureen watching and waving from the doorway.

Laughing about how quickly things were progressing, we made our way from our home in Smithville down the hill to the Grimsby Hospital, my hands held tightly to the seat as Glenn drove. "This time tomorrow, it'll all be over."

"You mean it will all be beginning."

As another contraction ripped through my body, the laughter and conversation came to a halt. I looked at the digital display on the dashboard and calculated it had been three minutes since my last contraction. "Better hurry."

Our second child, Caitlin, was in too much of a rush to wait for the doctor and decided to be born naturally, within minutes of arriving at the hospital. As I entered the front door, a wheelchair was slid under me.

"My wife is here to have a baby."

"How many minutes apart are her contractions?"

"Um … just a couple I think…."

Two nurses whisked me down the hall to Labour and Delivery. I couldn't tell you what they looked like, as my attention completely centred on my own task of bringing this new life into the world. The only thing I noticed was their white shoes dodging around obstacles as they quickly followed the olive green floor tiles, which were so shiny and clean they caught our reflection as we rushed down the hall. It was reassuring to see the sterile environment and feel the confidence of the nursing staff as they quickly assessed the situation and took control.

The change from clothing into a blue cotton gown was quick, and strings instead of buttons on the standard hospital garment made the whole process effortless. As one of the nurses took health information from Glenn, the other one helped me into a bed. "Now let's see how far along you are."

Under blinding lights in the small examining room, I saw Nurse One quickly look up from her examination and turn to the other nurse in the room. There was an edge to her voice and forced calm as she said, "Would you get on the phone and call the doctor? Tell him to come right away."

Before Nurse Two got back from making her phone call, Nurse One was already in place, to catch the eager new life. I reached down to confirm what I thought I felt. Sure enough, my fingertips met the top of the baby's head. We were on our own. There was no time to think about the dangers of this predicament.

In the movie *The Blue Lagoon*, the two main characters — a young boy and girl — are the sole survivors of a shipwreck. The young boy and girl grow up together on a deserted island, never being taught the facts of life and yet they find their way and conceive a child. Nine months later when the girl goes into labour, they think she is dying, *understandably*. They have no education on birthing a child, and yet nature runs its course and the child is born. They are shocked when a baby drops on the ground and also when it instinctively nuzzles its mother's breast to nurse. Although it is a fictional story, the premise is accurate — we have our animal instincts and they guide us, as much or more than our intellect.

It was Hobson's choice; there was no alternative. I was on primitive cruise control, nature took over, and I began to bear down — simultaneously, my hands reached down and pushed on my bulging stomach in a downward motion. I felt the baby move farther down the birth canal, from both the pressure I'd exerted with my abdominal muscles and my hands. I heard Glenn, beside me: "Don't!" And then the nurse, who said, "No, it's okay. Let her do what comes natural."

With the help of the nurse, Glenn and I delivered my second child, at 5:01 a.m. When the physician walked into the birthing room moments later, he could see the baby resting on top of my chest. With a big smile, he walked over to me. His question, "Well … is there anything left for me to do?" was met with the laughter that accompanies nervous relief.

Because of her swift delivery, I thought the baby had no time to be anything other than perfect, unlike her brother, who appeared with a temporarily misshapen head after so many hours in the birth canal — her perfect little head and seven-pound body appeared to me in a lovely shade of pink. Everything about her amazed me, from the top of her blonde hair to the tips of her tiny toes. Beauty quickly became her nickname, and she was, both inside and out. The cognitive dissonance kicked in once again, and I told myself I wanted a girl all along — a daughter to cherish. Once more, we had been blessed with a healthy child. I cried tears of joy for my daughter and gave thanks. I told her that I loved her to the sun and the moon and the stars and around the world and back again.

| Chapter 11 |

A few years later, my sister Maureen went into labour with her second child. When my mother called to say that Maureen was fine and didn't want anyone to come to the hospital, I said I understood. That's the way Maureen is — she never complains and she never asks for help, even when she needs it.

I couldn't help myself — I didn't listen to her request to be left alone. Without delay, I got in my car and drove to be with her. When I walked into her room, she smiled. She said nothing about her earlier desire to be left alone. Together, we monitored her contractions, and I stayed by her side. I had parked in the twenty-minute short-term parking with the intention of leaving when her husband arrived. Hours later, after her husband had arrived and I had a parking ticket, her baby was born. It was a wonderful experience for me to be there for the birth of my sister's child, to see her pain and her joy. I saw that beautiful little girl enter the world and be cradled in her father's arms for the first time. Witnessing this miracle moved me in a profound way. I knew I wanted another child.

I could not know that my third child would not live past a sixteen-week gestation period. Unlike my first two pregnancies, I felt horrible. I would struggle out of bed in the morning and my husband would take one look at my green face and tell me to go back to bed. He single-handedly took care of the children and the house for weeks. I lived on a diet of soda crackers and water.

We had picked out the names, Beth for a girl and Ben for a boy. I couldn't wait to see the baby that I knew we would call Beth. Once again, I went for an ultrasound. Anyone who has undergone this procedure can attest to the excitement of seeing her unborn child. It is well worth the discomfort of a full bladder, waiting for your name to be called, hobbling to the examining room, and baring your soul and body while a total stranger exerts pressure on your full abdomen — while you try not to wet your pants.

In the darkened room, I tried to get a look at the screen to see the baby, but the technician blocked my view. As in previous ultrasounds, I felt the plop of cold jelly on my tummy before the ultrasound wand moved over the area of the baby. The weight of the baby made it difficult for me to lie comfortably on my back, so I tried to bend my knees to relieve some of the strain. The technician was stern when she said, "Please straighten your legs."

Excited to be shown such things as the feet, the head, and the movement of the heart, I tried to catch a glimpse of the monitor, but the technician had no intention of sharing any wonders. Not a word was spoken. After what seemed like an unusually long time, the wand stopped moving. There was some clicking on the keyboard and then silence. "I'd like to try something else."

Handing me some tissues, she said, "Wipe off the excess gel. You can go and empty your bladder. Then come back and I would like to do an internal ultrasound."

In my two previous pregnancies, I had never been asked to do this. I hobbled to the washroom, and the relief of emptying my bladder was soon replaced with trepidation as I washed my hands and looked at myself in the mirror. *Everything is fine.* I couldn't shake the feeling of something being very wrong.

When I returned to the examination room, the technician was waiting. She was avoiding my eyes as I climbed back onto the examination table. An involuntary moan worked its way up my throat and escaped my mouth as I tried not to cringe and inch away from the intruding hands that repeated the exam internally. The keyboard clicked, the monitor beeped. The documentation was completed. The whole time not a word was spoken. None of the familiar "oohs" and "ahs" and pointing out of body parts. She just stared at the screen with a blank expression on her face. Her silence was terrifying. The tears ran down my cheeks but I didn't know why I was crying.

"All right we're all finished here, you can get dressed now." She moved away from me, turned the lights back on, and exited the room before I could think of what to say to her.

The next day my fears were confirmed when the doctor called with the results. "Diana, they were unable to find a heartbeat."

"What does that mean?"

"The baby has not survived. I'm sorry."

I couldn't believe it. Miscarriages happened to other people, not to me. I was healthy; I had done everything right — hadn't I? *There was that time I got the electrical shock in the kitchen, before the wiring was updated, was there anything else I was forgetting that might have harmed my child?*

I didn't want to add to my real or imagined list of transgressions in life by finding I had done something wrong. I always seemed to feel guilty about something, examining flaws in myself and wondering if I could have prevented events or changed outcomes. Whether it was through my actions or an awful twist of fate, my child had died.

I started moaning and dropped the phone, so my husband picked it up and spoke to the doctor. I sobbed an ugly cry while we learned what the X-rays confirmed, that the poor baby showed signs of spina bifida and was also hydrocephalic. She just didn't have the strength to survive.

We had loved her before she was even born. Our grief was overwhelming and our pain crushing. Inconsolable, I went to the hospital to be cared for and suffered massive haemorrhaging. I spent the night under medical care. The doctor suggested that I wait awhile before trying to conceive again.

I have never been very good at following orders. Three months later I was pregnant and we were expecting a December baby, a Christmas miracle.

For the next and longest nine months of my life, I worried about the safety of our unborn child. Every little hiccup was cause for alarm. I took good care of myself. I ate well, slept well, exercised, and took vitamins. I did not use creams, perfumes, hair dyes or even nail polish that could possibly enter my system and potentially harm my child. I prayed and I hoped. I didn't care if the baby had special needs, I promised my love unconditionally. Time couldn't pass fast enough. In the end, the birth of our fourth child proved to be the most challenging of them all, and would alter our lives forever.

| CHAPTER 12 |

1964

The Shadow of a girl has experienced many disappointments in her young life and nothing has turned out as she expected. She is no stranger to loss. Months after she marries, she learns of her father's suicide, and although she has not seen him in many years, it brings on a melancholy that she cannot shake. Although she has many bad memories of her father's drunken and erratic behaviour, she also remembers moments of frivolity and tenderness.

The following year she suffers a miscarriage. It breaks her heart. Every time she sees a baby, she feels like crying. She wonders, *Why me? What have I done to deserve this?* Her guilt is a constant companion. She takes care of herself and tries to conceive another child. She is successful, but after nine long months, the child dies at birth. In time, she gives birth to a third child, but it dies at the age of six weeks. She does not give up the hope of motherhood — she gives birth to a daughter and a son.

Although two of her children survive, her marriage does not.

| CHAPTER 13 |

Thursday December 16, 1993

I love Christmas. Nothing is more beautiful than the fresh, angelic, excited face of a child, no sound sweeter than that of pure, high voices singing Christmas carols and giggling through the lines of a school play.

Mothers and fathers, their winter coats draped behind them, are crammed into plastic chairs designed for children. They smile and wave at the other parents. A few people bravely squeeze down the treacherous aisles and between chairs, stepping on toes along the way, so they can momentarily visit with friends they haven't seen since the last assembly. Unlike the students who watched the Christmas pageant this afternoon, this largely adult audience is not chastised by the onlooking principal for their noise and chatter. It is beyond crowded, and although it is the dead of winter, the rising room temperature could warrant air conditioning. Decorations cut out of red and green construction paper adorn the walls of the school gymnasium, transforming it into an auditorium. Coffee and hot chocolate urns are stationed in the corner, ready to fill the Styrofoam cups that will be carried around and spilled on the floor after the performance. The overhead projector is setup at the back of the room, equipped to project words to the Christmas carols that will be sung off-key.

You can feel the anticipation in the air. Children are peeking out behind tattered blue curtains that hang unevenly across the stage. Costumes made from old pyjamas, towels, and belts are tugged into place but remain off-kilter. To us, the children couldn't be more precious.

Everyone strains to see in the dark concert hall and catch a glimpse of their family members. The parents smile broadly, with eyes for their child and theirs alone. This is a moment to be savoured. The fumbling of camcorders and cameras somehow takes away from the pleasure of the experience, but we just can't help ourselves. We are on a mission to capture the essence of the moment.

Predictably, the microphone will squeal as the principal fiddles with it in preparation for welcoming the families. There is always a child that sings the wrong words, a piano player that blunders a note, a missed step in the dance number, and a forgotten line in the nativity scene. At the end of the presentation, the children come by to say hello and hear how wonderful they were. If we're lucky, we may even be able to squeeze in a quick embrace without embarrassing them too badly, and if no one is looking, maybe even nuzzle our face in close enough to smell their scent.

There is not a word that can adequately express the passion we feel for our children. *Love* isn't a strong enough word to describe the immense feelings we have in our hearts — the love we carry for our children is so large that our bodies can't contain it. It oozes out of our pores, invades our thoughts, and affects every one of the decisions we make. When we introduce our children, "This is my *son*, or, this is my *daughter*," it's like rich chocolate rolling off of our tongue. You don't think anyone could possibly love their children as much as you love yours, but the reality is, of course they do.

2:00 p.m.

On this day, when I arrive home from my children's Christmas pageant, the glow of happiness and well-being still lingers. I walk into the kitchen to find my mother sitting at the breakfast nook.

Mom is a petite woman. She has beautiful, expressive light blue eyes. Although she likes to sing that she is "five-foot-two, with eyes of blue," she is actually five-foot-one. Mom is always well-buttoned-up in the latest fashion, with her hair perfectly groomed. Now I notice that she is wearing her nursing uniform. This tells me she has come right from work, and then it occurs to me that it is the middle of the day. She should still be at the office.

I stop humming the Christmas carol I can't seem to get out of my head. "Hey, what are you doing here?"

She doesn't answer the question — she asks one of her own. "Where have you guys been?"

"We were at the kids' Christmas pageant at the school."

"How was it?" I know my mother: she is stalling.

She continues talking about nothing when I know she has something important to say. From the many years in which we have lived, loved, and lost together, I can read from her speech and those expressive eyes, now avoiding mine, that something is wrong.

"What is it?"

"Diana, everything is all right...."

This confirms my suspicion that everything is definitely not all right. My worry increases when she forces a smile that doesn't reach her eyes.

"You are going to have your baby today."

Unless my mother has become psychic, as I have suspected on more than one occasion, there is only one way she could know this. My mother is a medical assistant in the same office as my physician, and she must have some evidence to substantiate this statement. Whatever she has heard, it can't be good. My mother has twelve grandchildren who refer to her as Grand-Mère. I am eight and a half months pregnant, and this baby will be her thirteenth grandchild.

"Diana, the doctor has been trying to get a hold of you."

My mind processes this statement at lightning speed, and the alarm bells start to go off in my head. "The results from the blood work you had yesterday show that your iron count is not what it should be. It's hard to know how long the levels have been so low."

"So low." That's worse than "not what it should be."

"The doctor thinks it would be a good idea to induce the labour."

What I hear is, *"Your iron is dangerously low — it has likely been this way for some time. The baby is not being nourished. The baby is in danger."*

Mom continues, "The doctor wants you to go to the hospital right away. She will meet you there and they will induce labour today."

It is December 1993 and I am scared.

In December 1992, I had the miscarriage that broke my heart.

In December 1991, my father died.

They say bad things come in threes, or is it the third time's the charm?

While my husband, Glenn, makes the arrangements for our other two children, Mom will take me to Joseph Brant Memorial Hospital in Burlington, where my doctor has delivery privileges. The doctor will meet us there. They will induce the labour today. It is two weeks before my due date.

| CHAPTER 14 |

1978

The land of opportunity has not been kind to the Shadow of a woman. It is a place where she can't seem to avoid disappointment, so she decides to make a new life for herself. She leaves her current home of Carson City in the Midwestern State of Michigan and crosses the border into Windsor, Canada. She has successfully adopted a new country and, in doing so, has invaded my world.

| CHAPTER 15 |

Thursday December 16, 1993
11:00 P.M.

Eight hours ago one of the nurses inserted an intravenous drip in my hand to stimulate labour. For most people, eight hours ends the work day, but for me the work is just beginning.

There are other beds in the room, but they are unoccupied, and I wonder why they have kept me isolated. It smells of hospital antiseptic and something distinctly medicinal that I can't put a name to. The lights are dim. The walls are painted muted and indistinct colours — even the scrubs the nurses are wearing are plain and patternless.

I encounter a strange combination of sensations that are difficult to distinguish. In the dark room, sounds echo as if coming through a long tunnel: the muted ding of an elevator, the creaking of a door before it latches closed, and varied footsteps, including one with an added swish, as if thighs or knees are rubbing together.

Conversations swirl around me, but they sound like they are far away. The faces of my husband and my mother fade in and out like waves on the shore. I hear their hushed exchanges and occasionally catch a couple words — *tired ... needs rest ... the baby ...* I'm not sure what is real and what I'm imagining, like when I'm sleeping and the phone ringing down the hall becomes part of my dream.

Although much time has passed, I don't seem to be making any progress. One of the nurses suggests to my family, "Why don't you go home and get some rest. I'm going to stop the drip and let her sleep for a few hours. We'll try again in the morning."

The drip stops. After a whispered "try and get some rest," Mom and Glenn leave for home, and I am left to wonder through the night what tomorrow will bring.

| CHAPTER 16 |

1991

The Shadow of a woman has been married for thirteen years to her second husband, a sixty-one-year-old man who was at one time married to her aunt. He is a police officer, and she learns the day-to-day activities of the police force.

During the latter part of their thirteen-year marriage, there is significant emotional and mental turmoil.

In her younger years, she would have never believed that she would turn to drinking for solace. Like her parents before her, alcohol has become her constant companion. She also would not have predicted that violence and confrontation would be a part of her everyday life, the sounds of crashing furniture and doors slamming a constant feature. She is strong, uncontrollable, and unpredictable. Due to her unstable and erratic behaviour, her husband lives in fear. There are nights when he barricades himself in the spare room, propping a chair up under the doorknob so that she won't be able to gain entry while he sleeps.

When her husband tells her he can't take any more and he wants a divorce, she is desperate to keep him and hatches a plan. The next time her husband leaves the house, she shaves her head. When he comes back a few hours later, she tells him she has cancer and has lost her hair to chemotherapy. Her husband is unsympathetic and also smarter than she thinks. Her bizarre behaviour is the last straw and he tells her she has a choice to make: either she leaves or he does.

Defeated, she leaves the comfortably furnished three-storey home with only the clothes on her back.

| CHAPTER 17 |

Friday December 17, 1993
3:00 P.M.

Twenty-four hours have passed. The doctor approaches and says, "I would like to give you a blood transfusion. It will raise your iron level and help to increase your strength." This makes me nervous; I've never had a blood transfusion, and I've read about people contracting some awful diseases from the procedure. You don't know who gave the blood — whether it was a man or a woman, a derelict or a scholar. I wonder if it matters. "Do you think I should?"

She replies, "It's ultimately your decision, but you're going to need your strength and the transfusion will help."

The donated bag of blood now hangs beside the recently replaced bladder of clear liquid that is keeping me hydrated.

The doctor — one of the few general practitioners who still deliver babies — is back at my side. She is medium height, slim, attractive, and has collar-length auburn hair with bangs. She is holding something resembling a large crochet hook. I don't like where this is going. She explains that the natural course of events has not taken place, and my water didn't break as expected before delivery — breaking the amniotic sac might speed up the labour. *Might* is the key word here, and it is that which resonates the strongest in my mind. No one asks for my opinion. The decision has been made. At this point, I don't care what they do as long as it works. The doctor snaps her latex gloves in place as she tries to prepare me. "Okay. Now, you will feel a little discomfort...."

"No shit."

Once the amniotic sac has been ruptured, the countdown begins. Doctors want to see your baby born as soon as six hours after this procedure, but there are cases where this interval lasts as long as twenty-four hours.

The discomfort becomes a reality as the menacing hook is inserted to break the membranes — water trickles down my body. I picture the amniotic fluid like a cushion of water surrounding my baby, and once it's gone, I imagine the baby crashing against my cervix without any padding.

I remember hearing somewhere that midwives discourage screaming during labour, but recommend moaning and grunting to relieve the pain. In the past I had heard other women scream out loudly during their labour and thought, *Is that really necessary?* I was wrong in thinking that I was superior. The truth was that I had just never been in the same position as those women. With this delivery, I am the one whose screams are heard down the corridors.

| CHAPTER 18 |

November 1993

The Shadow of a woman is once again in a disastrous relationship, now as the common-law wife of a nefarious criminal, and they are living together in a basement apartment in the city of Burlington in Ontario.

The woman applies for and receives welfare, which helps her to purchase the bottles of vermouth that she goes through daily. This regular consumption of alcohol leaves little funds for the other necessities of life and often fuels the fire of violence; the couple fight day and night. Thinking it will help to calm the storm, she has told a falsehood to her partner — that she is pregnant.

She goes to the local bank to open a new account. In the past she has used as many as fourteen different aliases and this time is no different. She provides a phoney name and a false occupation, writes down that she is a nurse working at Joseph Brant Memorial Hospital in Burlington. When she leaves the bank, she picks up the documents necessary to register the birth of a child so she will be able to obtain a birth certificate.

On her way home, she stops at the hospital. She walks in the front door and enters the gift shop to browse. Nearby, she sees the hospital directory and map and takes her time familiarizing herself with the layout of the building. From there she walks down to the cafeteria and gets a cup of coffee, smiling at staff and visitors as they pass her in the hall. She follows a lab technician through the cafeteria and notes every detail of the staff members' clothing, and as the technician moves into the greater area of the hospital, the woman, the Shadow, takes note of her daily protocol.

The Shadow passes the hospital library and pauses. When the technician is out of sight, she enters the library. She looks at the private empty room and smiles. The Shadow leaves the library, makes her way through the doors of the maternity ward, and stands looking through a glass window at the babies on the other side.

| CHAPTER 19 |

Saturday December 18, 1993
11:00 A.M.

Forty-four hours has passed. A petite blonde nurse does her routine check and confidently announces, "You are ten centimetres dilated. Time to have your baby." She calls the doctor in and there is a flurry of activity.

One of the nurses takes the sterile medical instruments and carefully places them beside me on a cart for the doctor. When the physician arrives, she says, "She's not ten centimetres, more like six. She's got a ways to go yet." As the doctor moves the cart back and peels off her gloves, I hear a quiet apology somewhere in the distance.

Are you shitting me?

My mom is back at my side. I look at her and we have a whole conversation without saying a word. She pats my leg.

2:30 P.M.

"She is ten centimetres dilated."

I don't think I have ever been so tired. The doctor confirms that we are finally there, as the baby has made its way down the birth canal and is ready to be born. It is time to push. Someone bends down low beside my head and speaks quietly and urgently in my ear. She is talking me through the tidal waves of each contraction. "Okay, Diana, another one is coming. Take a deep breath and ... push, push, push, push, push, push. Good."

Because of all of the concerns associated with this delivery, there has been no epidural given for pain management. I don't need to see the monitor the nurses are watching to know when another contraction is approaching — I can feel everything. The agony is fierce. With each spasm my body tenses as the pain tears down my spine like a bolt of lightning. The contractions squeeze my body like it is being put through an old wringer washing machine, twisting my organs on the way as they move on to my lower back and down my legs, each time leaving me exhausted and gasping for breath. One of the nurses wipes my brow with a cool cloth and then places ice chips in my mouth.

"You're almost there. Push, push, push, push. You can do it. Push, push, push, push, push."

I hear voices saying the baby is crowning, and the burning I feel as the baby eases its way out of the birth canal convinces me that they are right.

After an hour of pushing, at approximately 3:30 p.m., my baby enters this world. I have been waiting more than forty-eight hours to meet her: two thousand eight hundred and eighty minutes, over one hundred and seventy-thousand seconds.

The doctor proudly announces, "It's a girl."

I have another daughter. The doctor hands the baby over to my mother and refocuses her attention on me. My own voice is a whisper. "Is she okay?"

The doctor smiles. "Yes, she is fine, all ten fingers and all ten toes."

I look over to see my mom cradling the baby in her arms, a look of joy and wonder spread across her face. The baby is named Shelby Joan for her grand-mère, who helped to deliver her. She is nicknamed "Angel."

It was worth every minute and every second. I would do it all over again in a heartbeat to have this beautiful creature in my life. She is a gift I will never take for granted. After all the anxiety and all the distress, she is finally here and she is fine!

She will be okay now.

I can stop worrying.

She is safe.

Mom walking me down the aisle.

Exchanging vows.

Expecting Shelby.

| CHAPTER 20 |

December 1993

The Shadow of a troubled wife starts wearing maternity clothes and tells a number of people she is expecting. While at the local watering hole with her common-law husband, she tells people she has just come from the hospital, where she had an ultrasound that revealed she will have a baby girl within two weeks.

She goes from the hotel to her basement apartment and writes a list of nine baby names. The last name on the list is Shirley Megan, and it is written twice and underlined. She fills out the birth certificate that she obtained earlier in the week, and it is now ready to be filed.

When her husband returns home, he is in no mood for games, and an altercation ensues. They are soon involved in a shouting match. The landlady overhears a scuffle as furniture moves around and words turn to blows. The landlady hears, "Don't hit me! I'm eight and a half months pregnant."

In a drunken state, the husband attempts to leave the apartment. The Shadow of a wife punches, slaps, and scratches him while simultaneously tugging at his sleeve to make him stay. He eventually breaks free and leaves the apartment.

The Shadow has a drink to steady her nerves and leaves shortly after to make her way to Joseph Brant Memorial Hospital in Burlington.

| CHAPTER 21 |

"No!"

It is time for the third stage of labour: the delivery of the placenta. The placenta has ruptured and only partially delivered, and my attempts to push the remaining piece of the placenta from the birth canal are futile. The metallic smell of blood is in the air, and I see it on the person in front of me. Hands are everywhere, first in me and then on me, pushing down with all their might on my abdomen. As I fight to push the doctor and nurses off me, I scream bloody murder. The pressure they are exerting on my already aching, bruised body is unbearable. My cries are heard down the halls by the other mothers. I wonder if they are thinking, *Is that really necessary?*

The doctor remarks, "Maybe I better put you under."

I breathe a sigh of relief as the hands are removed from my body, and I thank God for small mercies. The doctor calls for an anaesthesiologist, and soon I am blissfully unconscious as they remove the placenta.

After an indeterminate period of time, the marathon is finally over, and I have been moved to a recovery room. I am shivering uncontrollably. At regular intervals, the light blanket covering my trembling body and wrapped snugly around my feet is removed and replaced with a warm one. I wonder where this seemingly endless supply of warm green blankets is coming from, and I picture a huge clothes dryer continually operating around the corner.

When my husband reaches for my hand, I ask, "Please call everyone and tell them not to come up to see me tonight. I don't feel very well."

Glenn calls my sisters and brother and tells them to stay home, that I need my rest, and that they can come and visit tomorrow. Maureen agrees, then bundles up and, without delay, gets in her car and drives to the hospital. A short while later, I look over through an oxygen mask and think I see my sister. I'm not sure if I'm dreaming, or if she has ignored my request just as I ignored hers in the past. Sure enough, she is standing beside me and reaches out to me. With tears streaming down her face, she says, "I had to come."

I think, *God, I'm glad she's here.*

| Chapter 22 |

Thursday December 23, 1993
11:45 A.M.

Shelby Joan is five days old. I have watched a variety of mothers come and go during my five days in this room. Though the women are different, there is a similar pattern to their behaviour. I have seen them watching their babies in wonder, falling in love as they change, bathe, and feed them. The mothers in the other three beds have slept with their newborns beside them in bassinets, eagerly reaching over and retrieving them whenever their cherubs made the slightest sound of distress.

The first three nights of Shelby's life were spent behind the glass window of the nursery under the watchful eye of the nursing staff.

The large amount of blood I lost, my low hemoglobin levels, and the unexpected surgery I endured to remove the placenta had left me unable to care for Shelby around the clock. The nurses brought Shelby to me when she needed to be fed, with strict orders to stay in bed while I held her. After fainting during a short walk across the room to the washroom, I gladly complied with their requests.

My body has now had time to heal. For the past two days, I have had the pleasure of having Shelby at my side full-time. I have been able to relish in caring for her, feeding, bathing, and changing her like the other mothers. Although I still feel weary, I have no desire to put her back in her little bed.

I am cuddling with my little bundle of joy, covering her face with soft kisses and marvelling at the wonder of creation. She smells like all things good: baby powder, fresh air, and sunshine. I twist her tuft of cornsilk hair between my fingers and look at her soft pink skin and heart-shaped mouth. I admire the big round eyes, a gift from her grand-mère, and their shade of chocolate-brown, a gift from her deceased grandfather. I could watch her for hours.

I look up and see Glenn entering the door to my room with our two older children. My heart warms at this picture of the man that I have loved since high school, walking with one hand in my son's the other in my daughter's. Our eyes connect and I feel the immense closeness created by this shared experience of having a child.

Michael and Caitlin are looking for me and the baby as they enter.

"There she is — I see her." Michael is in big brother mode and points across the room. Big smiles spread across their faces and their footsteps speed up.

"Hi Mama, can I hold the baby?" Caitlin asks.

"Me too, I want to hold the baby."

After hugs and kisses, Michael and Caitlin hastily discard their little winter coats and hats beside my bed and crawl up on a blue vinyl hospital chair. Their little legs are so short that they dangle over the edge of the chair without reaching the floor. Baby Shelby is propped up, oh so carefully, in their arms, with Glenn never more than inches away, ready to spring to the rescue. Michael and Caitlin take turns gently cradling the new member of the family, while I snap pictures of them all together. Glenn and I make the predictable statements: "Watch her head." "Be very careful."

The children are so proud that they are big enough to hold their baby sister. I have given them both little Treasure Trolls as a present; Michael's troll has blue hair and wears a yellow T-shirt that reads I'M A BIG BROTHER. Caitlin's troll has pink hair and matching T-shirt, proclaiming I'M A BIG SISTER.

The children stare down into Shelby's tiny face and examine her closely. Their comments are precious: "She has really little fingers." Michael doesn't realize his were once that small.

"Can I see her feet?" Caitlin pulls at the receiving blanket covering Shelby's toes.

"She's looking at me." Michael smiles at Caitlin.

"Can she see me?" Caitlin asks her father.

"I think she just smiled," Michael informs me.

They hear a few bodily functions occurring inside the baby's diaper. There are giggles and smirks.

Shelby is back in her father's arms, and the children's attention is shifted back to me. I am inundated with the events of the day.

"Michael got dressed today and there was a sock stuck to the back of his shirt," Caitlin says with a laugh.

"Dad saw it before we left and took it off." He turns around to show the back of his green Ninja Turtles sweatshirt. "See."

I listen to their very animated stories and picture things back at home. I am ready to be back in my own house and feel the comfort of familiarity — it seems like an eternity since I left for the hospital. I smile, thinking how concerned I was that day and how everything worked out in the end.

Their visit nearing an end, the children crawl up on the bed for an embrace. "Bye Mama, I love you."

And with all my heart, I reply with what I believe to be true, "I love you more."

After their visit, Glenn intends to bring them Christmas shopping and then to his mother's, who will watch them while he comes back for me this afternoon, once I have seen the doctor and am officially released.

When he brings the children back from their grandma's, it will be a great big surprise for them to find me and their new baby sister waiting for them at home. Tonight will be a quiet family night: I imagine popcorn popping and books being read in front of the fireplace while excited looks drift to the brightly decorated Christmas tree and the stockings waiting to be filled. Tomorrow is Christmas Eve, and we are looking forward to the celebrations with our family.

We plan to attend an open house that the relatives on my side are hosting. We will enter my brother's home like a circus troupe, juggling children, presents, preparations for the food table, and contributions to the cooler full of beer and wine. During welcoming embraces under the mistletoe, there will be mass confusion as coats, food, gifts, and drinks change hands in the crowded foyer. This will be Shelby's first Christmas, and no doubt she will sleep through most of the chaos as she travels from one set of arms to another.

Mom will have baked her traditional tourtière meat pies, complemented with gravy and canned peas. Chuck and his wife, Beverly, will have prepared a variety of dips and cheeses to enjoy with crusty loaves of bread and crackers. Salty chips, nuts, and pretzels will constantly be replenished in their small Christmas serving bowls. The fruit and vegetables laid out will not receive the same attention as the deliciously rich high-fat foods, but the fact that they are included warrants credit. After much snacking, reminiscing, laughter, affection, singing and guitar playing, we will attend midnight Mass and remember the reason for the season and thank God that we have been so truly blessed.

The gathering with Glenn's side of the family the following morning will also give new meaning to the word *bedlam*. When we stop by his parents' house, there will be a topsy-turvy collection of children's toys. With not enough room under the tree, the wrapped presents for twenty grandchildren will spread out to cover the living room floor in a holy mess. There will be utter pandemonium as they dive into their presents to discover Slinkies, Etch A Sketches, Mr. Potato Heads, dolls, trucks, colouring books, and other such wonders. That kind of chaos is calming in its normalcy and predictability. Glenn's mom, Patricia, and his father, Patrick, will be sitting in their wingback chairs. Patricia will be laughing at the children while Patrick tries to look gruff, though he is equally enjoying the frivolity. The smell of turkey and homemade pies and bread will permeate the house, and the hard-working oven will raise the temperature in the house to the point where we are removing our sweaters.

As I am thinking of the festivities ahead, Glenn leans over and kisses me. He whispers in my ear, "See you soon." The children wave as they exit, and Glenn turns to wink at me before he takes his leave. As their steps fade away, I can hear their little angelic voices excitedly asking questions.

All is right with my world.

| CHAPTER 23 |

Thursday December 23, 1993
12:00 P.M.

The Shadow of a criminal enters the front door of Joseph Brant Memorial Hospital. She knows the layout of the building and goes directly to the library. Here, she removes her winter coat and leisurely drops it over a chair. Next, she discards her sweater, revealing a hospital smock and her casual slacks. Inside of her pants pocket is a piece of paper with the printed words MEETING IN PROGRESS. She opens the door to the hallway and takes a cursory look, checking that no one is walking by, then posts the sign. Once back inside the library, she removes a bag stashed in her coat. It contains a colourful baby blanket and a blue sleeper that zips up the middle — both are folded neatly and placed under the winter coat.

The Shadow exits the library and heads to the lab. Glancing in the door, she sees a couple of technicians. One of the staff is on the phone and barely notices as she enters. The second girl is sorting through some papers on the counter and looks up to smile at the infiltrator. The Shadow catches her eye and tells the medical staff that she has forgotten her lab coat and needs one to go in a patient's room. The lab technician offers to loan her a spare coat and quickly retrieves one from an adjacent room. With a thank you and a smile, the Shadow leaves the lab.

She buttons up the smock as she's walking and puts on a pair of latex gloves. There is no turning back. She heads for the maternity ward to look for the baby girl who will soon become her daughter. She will name her Shirley Megan.

| CHAPTER 24 |

December 23, 1993
12:20 P.M.

Breastfeeding in the movies is so effortless, even romantic. In reality, there is a learning curve to the art of nursing a child. The nurses say that when your milk "first comes in," it can be a little overwhelming. That's the understatement of a lifetime. I was always well-endowed, but I now feel like Chesty Morgan. When I roll over, I feel like I am dragging two ten-pound bowling balls with me. The kind nurses have tried packing my upper body in ice to help ease the discomfort, and it provides momentary relief. A wonderful lactation consultant has assisted me in the art of breastfeeding, sharing important tips with me I had forgotten from previous nursing experiences. She has also suggested that I take off my clothes and cuddle the baby skin to skin under the blankets while nursing. What a great idea. Late at night, when the room is dark, I have done just that.

Now, as I nurse Shelby, I could float away with the fulfillment. The sense of closeness is indescribable. My eyes well — my happiness is overflowing. This child that is a part of me has filled my heart. I am content and at peace, knowing that I have the rarest and most wonderful of Christmas gifts. Nothing exists in time and space except the two of us. I gently push her soft wispy hair back from her forehead as I lean down to kiss her beautiful innocence. My lips linger as I savour the feel of her velvet skin.

There are presently three mothers recovering in this room, which is equipped to handle four patients — the woman across from me has just cheerfully left for home with her smiling husband and sleeping newborn. I am in the bed closest to the window, and the curtain is drawn on my opposite side, separating me from the mother in the bed beside me. I hear the sound of footsteps entering the room. A lumbering shadow shuffles back and forth on the other side of the curtain.

The Shadow speaks with the mother beside me. The sound of hushed voices fills my ears. I continue to focus on my baby but catch a few comments from their conversation:

"Oh, it's a boy?"

"How is he doing?"

"How are you feeling?"

The conversation ends abruptly as the Shadow slithers to the other side of the room and speaks with another patient, but again I can't see the interloper. I only hear her comments:

"A baby boy?"

"Well, this is the room for boys, isn't it?"

"Is this your first child?"

"How old is he?"

The lighting in the room has shifted; the sun rests behind a cloud. The walls, which were white, are now a shade of grey.

Shelby lies content, feeding on my milk. Her soft scent fills the air. I feel a presence lurking close to my bed, and I look up to find a slovenly nurse glancing at the name card on the bassinet. She looks at me with weathered eyes. She is *the Shadow*. She forces a brisk smile that has no mirth.

"You've had a daughter, how lovely ... And how is ... Shelby doing?"

"She's fine."

The woman deliberates for what seems like an eternity. Her eyes slowly crawl across my bed and reach Shelby. She smiles awkwardly as she smoothes her dishevelled hair. I feel uncomfortable and annoyed; I just want to be alone with my child. It seems to me these routine checks have become redundant. The woman keeps her attention on my child while she speaks. "We have to take her for some blood work."

"Again? Didn't you get enough before?"

This will be the third time they have drawn blood from Shelby. Her little foot still wears the bandages from the previous needle pricks.

"Well ... no ... we didn't ... so I am going to take her down to the lab. That way if we don't get everything we need, we can just repeat the tests there."

"Can you come back later? I'm going to be awhile."

"That's okay. I'll just wait for you to finish."

She turns her back to me and glances out the window as if she has all the time in the world. The sun retreats farther behind the body of clouds in response to her gaze.

Doesn't she have something else to do, somewhere else to be? I am frustrated because I feel like I should hurry, but there are some things you just can't rush. There is something about her I don't like — I want to tell her to go away, but I don't want to be rude.

Someone from housekeeping comes in and sterilizes the recently vacated bed across from me. For some reason the two hospital staff members do not acknowledge one another. I notice the smell of disinfectant and it overpowers the beautiful baby smells of moments earlier.

Ten minutes later housekeeping has left and the Shadow is still standing at the window with her back to me. She has not said anything since she turned around and is unusually still; her silhouette is a stone statue.

It seems like she has eyes in the back of her head, though she is probably just watching my reflection in the glass window, for she turns when I am finished and reaches for my baby before I have even had a chance to cover myself back up. I don't want to hand her over.

I hand her over. "Maybe I should burp her first."

She mutters, "I don't think I'll take that" as she glances at the bassinet. And then she speaks as if she has just had the greatest idea: "I'll just carry her, and I can burp her while I'm walking." She holds Shelby against her chest and abruptly turns to leave, saying, "I'll be back in twenty minutes." She looks back at me over her shoulder as she's walking away. "Don't worry; I'll take good care of her." I hear the squeak of her footsteps as she makes her exit.

My daughter's big brown eyes stare into mine, and I watch them as every step takes her a little farther away from me. I watch until she is out of sight.

After they turn the corner, I think I hear a baby cry. I wonder if I should walk out to the hallway to check if it's *my* baby. I think of Shakespeare's *Macbeth* and a famous quotation spoken by one of three witches: "By the pricking of my thumbs, something wicked this way comes."

I don't follow my instincts. I shake it off as a combination of fatigue and an overly active imagination.

| CHAPTER 25 |

December 23, 1993
12:35 P.M.

The Shadow of an impostor walks out of the maternity ward with a baby girl.

She is relieved and satisfied. *It was easy*, she thinks, so easy.

She pushes the button for the elevator. There are a couple of people who look at her curiously. The Shadow avoids any conversation and keeps the tightly wrapped baby out of their direct line of vision. After the Shadow exits the elevator, she goes to the hospital library. She opens the door with the sign that reads MEETING IN PROGRESS and then locks it securely behind her.

She methodically changes the baby out of her hospital gown and into the blue sleeper that she stashed in the library earlier in the morning.

The baby, recently fed, is drowsy. The Shadow watches as the baby's head tilts back and she falls asleep.

"What a good girl, Shirley Megan," the Shadow coos in her ear.

The Shadow wraps the baby in a new colourful blanket. After putting on her winter coat, the Shadow tries to tuck the baby inside, but the infant will not fit. The Shadow decides to just carry the baby out in her arms. There is no reason to be concerned; she has done nothing wrong — it is her child, after all. Exiting the library, she reaches up and removes the sign before proceeding up to the first floor.

Surveillance cameras at the hospital record the woman approaching the front exit of the hospital. Cameras show a few people look at the woman with a baby in her arms and then look back at one another. They lean together and whisper something as they watch the Shadow of a criminal leave the hospital with an infant in her arms. The Shadow exits the front door at exactly 12:54:47 with a child that does not belong to her.

| CHAPTER 26 |

December 23, 1993
12:40 P.M.

I have some severe abdominal cramping, which momentarily distracts me from thinking of the blood work being done at the lab. My gurgling stomach is the result of a decision I made earlier this morning, when I was visited by one of the nurses and asked a round of routine questions.

"How is your pain level?"

"All right."

"On a scale of one to ten, ten being the worst, what number would you choose for how much pain you are in?"

"Four."

"Would you like something for the pain?"

I would like something … but all that codeine can't be helping.
"No thank you."

"Have you had a bowel movement yet?"

"No." The same answer I have given for five days — I know what the next question will be.

"Would you like an enema?"

Geez does anyone actually answer yes to that question? At my lack of response, the nurse continues. "It's your choice, but it's not a good idea to let it go too long — any extra strain could cause added problems and discomfort."

"That's some choice."

The nurse is not amused. She adds, "You really should consider it."

"Okay, I probably should."

The nurse is petite. She reminds me of the female movie star Linda Hunt, who once played a man in the film *The Year of Living Dangerously*. Everything about her is short; her legs, her arms, and even her fingers are like those of a child. She brushes her short brown hair from her eyes and begins to unpack her supplies. I am drawn to her hands, which are very tiny but unmistakably capable.

The procedure is surprisingly simple and fast but undeniably humiliating. I say, "Well that was pleasant," and instantly regret my remark. The nurse doesn't respond to my comment with what I'm sure she is thinking: *Imagine how I feel.*

The nurse packs up her things. "Stay put for the allotted time. You will feel like you have to go sooner, but don't."

Easier said than done — the seconds tick by slowly and the discomfort increases quickly. I look at my watch and only three minutes have passed, so I try to distract myself by remembering the entire lyrics to a song, a method I often use when I have to pass the time. "I've Just Seen a Face" pops into my head, and I start singing the music in my mind. There is something beyond my physical malaise that is bothering me, but I can't put my finger on what it is, so with that thought slightly out of reach, I sing of a face that I can't forget.

Now I try to remember the album the song is from and the order of the soundtrack. Beatles, *Help!* album, side two, followed by … "Yesterday." I hum aloud of troubles that I wish would go away and of how yesterday seemed much easier.

The music does help and I make it to ten minutes. When it's all over, I have to admit that the nurse was right; I feel better. Now when I go home, I won't have anything to worry about.

I decide to freshen up and pack up my few belongings. As I walk to the sink in the washroom, I glance over at the other mothers who are resting peacefully and we share a smile. I don't want to intrude on their moment and no words are exchanged. Except for the barely perceptible hum of the fluorescent lights and the occasional cooing of the two babies in the room, it is quiet.

I brush my hair and put it in an elastic band, then close my eyes and lather up my face with soap and water. While splashing water on my face to rinse off the soap, I hear a single set of footsteps enter the room and stop abruptly. I stop mid-splash and listen more carefully. There's something curious in the way that the footsteps have stopped. The sounds through the bathroom door are muffled, but I sense urgency in the hushed exchanges that follow. I quickly rinse my face, and as I am reaching for a towel, I hear a question through the door. It's a question that carries a note of concern: "Diana, do you have the baby in there with you?"

Suddenly, I don't feel so well.

"No … They took her for blood work?" I think back and can't decide whether I've made a statement or posed a question.

The movement outside my door has ceased, as have the voices. I look at myself in the mirror and I'm alarmed not only by the stillness outside of my door but by the fear I see in my own face.

I slowly open the door to find a nurse on the threshold, looking at me intently. The silence builds and her eyes grow much too wide. "Who took her for blood work?"

There it is again, that hint of alarm. As my skin begins to prickle, a flush spreads up to my face. "The nurse...."

"Which nurse?" Her face tells me that she is not going to like my answer no matter what I say, and I'm feeling increasingly sick.

There is an awkward pause and I'm embarrassed when I answer. "I don't know."

She stares at me hard for a moment — turns and leaves the room. Only my eyes move as she walks to the nurses' station outside my door.

"Does anyone know anything about blood work being ordered for baby Shelby?"

I walk to a spot where I have a better view of the nursing station. My hearing has become incredibly acute. A nurse picks up the phone and dials a number, and I can hear the questions being asked but not the answers. "Hello, I'm calling to check on blood work that was ordered for a patient."

I want to believe that everything is all right — I can't convince myself that it is. I start begging in my head, *Please, please ...*

"Hello, this is maternity calling, do you have an infant at the lab for tests?"

The nurse looks at me and turns her back to continue her conversation, but with her voice lowered, and while I can no longer make out her words, her body language gives her away: she's scared.

No, no, no ...

She hangs up the phone and is very still. *Oh God ... Say they're on their way back, say everything is fine.*

When she turns around, she is biting her lower lip pensively. She walks back into the room, and her eyes are glossy with what looks like unshed tears. She says the words that will haunt me for the rest of my life: "Diana ... no blood tests were ordered."

It echoes in my troubled mind. "No blood tests were ordered."

It hits me like a jolt of electricity: I have just made the biggest mistake of my life. The blood is rushing in my ears. I hear a moaning sound like an animal and realize it is coming from me.

My hands move to my abdomen and I take a very deep breath — in my nose — and slowly blow it out of my mouth before I say, "Call the police." *This can't be happening. This can't be happening.*

No one answers me. There is a flurry of activity around me. Some other nurses enter the room and everyone seems to be asking questions but no one has the answers. The two other mothers in the room don't say a word as they look on in terror, likely thinking, "That could have been me. Thank God that's not me." One of the mothers is holding her baby tightly. The other mother has her hand over her mouth and is reaching toward the bassinet where her child sleeps.

I don't know what to do. I don't know where to look, and my eyes dart around the room as I pace back and forth like a caged animal. "Not this, not my baby, anything but this." Cold fear is engulfing me, swallowing me up whole like a powerful tidal wave. *This is a mistake. Any minute now that nurse is going to walk around the corner holding Shelby. She is going to hand her back over to me and I am going to tell Glenn how I had the most awful scare today.*

Time passes. People come and go. The hospital staff continues their calls to try and discover what has happened to Shelby. The background noise is a steady hum of voices. As I pace the room, an announcement comes over the hospital public address system: "Attention all staff, we have a code yellow." This signifies a *missing* patient.

With dread I think that there are a lot of floors and rooms in this hospital. I try to remember the number of buttons in the elevator to try to work out how many floors there are, but I can't remember. I recall hearing someone say there are over four hundred beds in the hospital, but I have no idea how many rooms this equates to. *Shelby is in one of those rooms. This is all a big mistake. Most of the things we worry about never happen.... Most of the things we worry about never happen.*

One of the nurses comes into the room accompanied by the hospital chaplain. With her wingman in place, she tells me —

with forced gentleness — they have no idea where Shelby is. "She is not in the lab and no one in the hospital seems to know where she might be."

I ask her again if the police have been called, and she says she believes that they have been. I have yet to see them and wonder why they are not here.

Amidst the chaos outside my door, I hear the familiar voice of someone who is being prevented from entering. "I'm here to see Diana."

"This is really not a good time to visit."

It has just occurred to me how alone I am. I dash into the hall to see my sister Debbie with a nurse's arm around her shoulder, and it looks as though she is being directed away from me — my sister Debbie, one of my best friends and a member of my club of five. I see her curly brunette hair and the confusion in her big brown eyes. I see the big leather purse draped over her shoulder and the brightly painted Christmas tin filled with gourmet popcorn in her arms. I pounce on her and literally drag her toward my room. "This is my sister, she stays!"

My sister, who has four children of her own, has just driven two hours in a snowstorm to see me. In her eyes I see alarm, confusion, and fear. She has not spoken a word. She is just staring at my dilated pupils as I claw at her and try to remove her dark bulky coat. *Maybe if I take her coat she won't leave.* Before her coat is fully unbuttoned, she drops it to the floor, where it pools at her feet — she steps out of it while she continues to watch me. I take her hands in mine and hold on for dear life. "She took my baby."

"She took my sweet baby."

| CHAPTER 27 |

Fear bubbles inside of me and escapes like steam through a whistling kettle. It travels down the hall, infecting everyone in its path. A tableau of foreboding unfolds in front of me. A startled woman in a blue hospital gown peeks out of her door to see what is happening; beside her she drags a squeaky pole that carries her intravenous. A hunched-over patient, who is in labour, stops pacing the corridor to look up in alarm.

The nurse who greeted Debbie realizes that we are upsetting the other patients. While looking over her shoulder, she now ushers Debbie and I back into the hospital room and away from curious onlookers. "Come this way, please."

The only words I can find to say are "She took my sweet baby."

Once we are back in my hospital room, the nurse shuts the door behind us and turns to Debbie, saying what I cannot — her words come slowly, almost apologetically, "The baby is missing."

"MISSING?" Debbie looks from the nurse to me and then back at the nurse.

Now the nurse's words speed up, playing back like a music box that is wound too tightly. With one breath she outlines the situation: "We're not sure where the baby is … Someone came and took her for blood work. We have no record of any tests being scheduled for today and no one at the lab knows anything about blood work being processed." A thin layer of perspiration glows on the nurse's forehead, and she wipes it with the sleeve of her scrubs.

"Did you call the police?" asks Debbie.

The nurse nods. Yes.

"Does Glenn know?"

I shake my head. No.

Everything has happened so quickly. I haven't had time to process the logistics of it or think about whom I should call or what I should do. Glenn doesn't know any of this. The thought of him not knowing is sobering. The thought of the pain he is soon going to feel when he hears what has transpired since he left makes me sick to my stomach. *Oh God, Oh God….*

"Where is he?" Debbie picks up the phone and dials nine to get an outside connection.

Glenn is supposed to be at his mother's, dropping off our children. I picture them jumping for joy and telling their grandma about everything that happened at the mall while Glenn looks on with a smile. "He should be at his mom's." I rhyme off the numbers.

Debbie looks at me while she waits for the connection to be made. There is silence until she says, "The line is busy." She puts the phone back in the receiver for only a moment to break the connection and immediately picks it back up and redials the numbers. I hear the sound of each key as it is pressed. Each number has its own unique sound — a musical keyboard, the soundtrack of disaster. "The line is still busy."

We remain standing, she with the phone in her hands, and me with my heart in mine. I have to keep moving, as the nervous energy propels me forward. Shuffling from one foot to the other, my mind races — I have an idea. "Call the operator and have them break into the line."

"Can they do that?"

"I'm sure they do that." I'm not sure at all. In fact, I have no idea. I saw that in a movie once.

I raise my eyebrows and quickly nod to emphasize how sure I am.

Debbie does as ordered and dials zero. "Hello, operator? I have been trying to reach a line and it has been busy for hours."

It has actually been minutes, but I fully support the exaggeration. Debbie looks at me as I continue to nod in encouragement.

Forcefully, she states, "This is an emergency! I have to reach the person on the line that is busy."

"What is the number you are trying to reach?"

I say the numbers again, and Debbie repeats them to the operator. The operator confirms them as she dials. It's an echo of numbers: "664 ... 664 ... 664 ..." After all seven numbers are validated, the operator is able to make the connection and join the call already in progress.

Glenn's mother, Patricia, is on the phone, and the operator interrupts her conversation, though we are not privy to the words that follow. "Hello, this is the operator. You have an important call, please hang up the phone and I will connect you."

Not realizing the magnitude of this statement, Patricia disregards the message and continues her chat.

Her friend, Mrs. Duncan, inquires, "What was that all about?"

"I don't know, probably some mix-up."

Mrs. Duncan is one of Patricia's prayer partners and they continue to discuss attending services together this week.

I am looking over at Debbie and wondering what is taking so long. Seconds stretch into minutes. "What's happening?"

Debbie shrugs and shakes her head. As I am contemplating putting my ear beside hers to eavesdrop, I hear my sister ask, "Operator, have you been able to get through?"

"Yes, I've asked them to hang up but they are still talking. I'll try again." The operator interrupts the conversation once again. "Please hang up the phone. I have an important call waiting to be put through to you."

Patricia decides to wrap things up. "I better go and see what this is all about. I'll talk to you later."

"Okay, Patricia, I'll talk to you later."

As soon as she hangs up the phone, it rings and she answers. "Hello?"

My sister is finally connected with Patricia. I see her take a deep breath. She clears her throat before saying, "Patricia, this is Diana's sister Debbie. Is Glenn there?"

"He's not here, but he should be back anytime now. He and Mary took the kids shopping."

How do you tell a grandmother that her grandchild has been kidnapped? "I am at the hospital with Diana. There is a problem here and we need to find Glenn."

She now has Patricia's full attention. "The baby has been ..." She looks over at me, and pauses. She tries again. "The baby ... The baby is missing...."

There, that sounds better.

"... What did you say?"

"The baby is missing."

"Oh blessed hour!"

"Please tell Glenn to come back to the hospital right away."

Debbie hangs up and we stare at each other for a moment before she says, "She'll tell him."

| CHAPTER 28 |

December 23, 1993
12:54 P.M.

At 12:54 p.m. the hospital administration calls 911 and notifies the local police department of a missing patient at the Joseph Brant Memorial Hospital. The police advise the hospital management to put the building in lockdown, but it is too late.

12:54:47 P.M.

The Shadow of a kidnapper exits the hospital. She leaves the property and walks to a nearby condominium complex and starts randomly pushing buttons. When a woman answers on the speaker, the Shadow explains that she was trying to reach a friend in the building and is stranded with her newborn child. The kind-hearted woman offers to drive the stranger and her baby to the bus station in town.

From the bus station, the kidnapper takes a bus to the Zellers department store on the other side of town. She inquires where the washroom is and goes in with the baby. There, she throws away the borrowed lab coat from the hospital. In the pocket of the lab coat are the latex gloves she was wearing, syringes, and Vacutainers for collecting blood. She also scrunches up the MEETING IN PROGRESS sign that she still has in her pocket and throws it in the garbage.

In the main aisle of the store, there is a display of children's knapsacks and school supplies. Selecting a dark navy backpack with no markings, she removes the tags and places the baby inside.

A couple of teenagers notice the strange behaviour. "Did you see what that lady just did?"

The Shadow makes her way to the children's department and selects a few baby outfits, which she brings to the checkouts. With her packages and backpack in hand, the Shadow uses the phone at the exit, and the local taxi company quickly answers the direct line. When the taxi arrives, the Shadow gets into the front seat and drops the knapsack, containing the baby, on the floor between her feet.

The driver thinks it's strange, but he doesn't dwell on it — he has seen a lot of strange things over the years. He brings his passenger to the basement bachelor apartment that she shares with her common-law husband and leaves after collecting his fare. The apartment is not locked, and when the door swings open, her eyes must adjust to the darkness inside. The two small windows inside are covered with faded curtains. She stands listening for a moment. There is the unmistakeable feeling of emptiness. She is alone.

The small kitchenette opens up to a living area with a small dresser and a worn green pullout couch, which is covered with an old blanket. She puts the pile of infant's clothing that she has purchased on the dresser, then opens a drawer to retrieve a pen and paper. She sits down only long enough to write a note: "Husband, take what you want. I wish you happiness inside your bottle. Merry Christmas, Your Wife and Daughter."

| CHAPTER 29 |

When Glenn and Mary pull into his mother's driveway to drop off the children after shopping, he has no idea what awaits him. His mother is standing with the door flung open, the brisk air slapping her face. He looks at her and wonders why she is standing in the cold. "Mom?"

During the children's cheerful hellos and embraces, Glenn looks on curiously. Careful to make sure the children can't hear what she is saying, his mother quietly passes on Debbie's message. "Debbie called from the hospital."

"Debbie called?"

"Yes, she said the baby is missing."

Her body exhibits the same tension that her voice conveys. She clutches her rosary beads in her hands. Glenn and his sister, Mary, look at each other. "Missing ... What is that supposed to mean?"

Glenn's mother has a hearing impairment, and he thinks she must have misunderstood the phone conversation, that maybe there is some sort of medical problem. All kinds of possibilities are running through his head. *Maybe someone told her that the heartbeat is missing. Maybe some medical documents are missing. Surely, they couldn't have misplaced a child.*

"They can't find the baby. You have to go to the hospital."

His eyes, the windows to his soul, show concern. His voice reflects anger. "What are you talking about, I was just there and everything was fine!"

"You have to go to the hospital, the baby is missing."

Getting louder, he repeats, "What are you talking about?"

Mary reaches for the keys gripped tightly in his hand. "Let's go. I'll drive."

Leaving the children inside with their grandmother, Glenn heads back to the car, refusing to relinquish the keys. He is nearly out of the driveway when Mary jumps into the passenger seat to join him. It is fourteen kilometres to the hospital, but the fifteen-minute drive feels like an eternity. As they drive, Mary tries to comfort her brother: "I'm sure it's just an honest mistake.... Everything will be fine once we get there."

He does not respond, and she makes no further effort at conversation.

They drive through the heart of Stoney Creek and onto the highway that will lead them to the Skyway Bridge — a massive structure that their father, an iron worker, helped to build. It spans the harbour on Lake Ontario and is a means to travel from Stoney Creek to Burlington, where the hospital is. On a more personal level, the bridge usually serves as a marker of the final stretch when returning home from a holiday. Now, it provides Glenn and his sister with a clear view of the hospital and the flashing lights from a barrage of police cruisers and fire engines, evoking only a feeling of foreboding.

As they take the off-ramp to Burlington, traffic comes to a halt. Barriers are being constructed not only at the hospital but on all the streets and ramps surrounding it. Glenn and Mary gaze in disbelief at the evidence of a catastrophe in plain view. There is no suppressing the sense of emergency, yet they still feel a sense of unreality in knowing that this situation has anything to do with them.

As they pull into the hospital entrance, Mary and Glenn see police officers stopping every vehicle leaving the premises and systematically searching through car interiors and trunks, as well as miscellaneous packages. Glenn takes a sharp turn to enter the parking lot and the car comes to an abrupt halt, then he flings open his door and sprints to the entrance, leaving Mary behind to park the vehicle.

Inside the hospital, there is a lineup of people waiting to exit. Each person trying to leave is being asked to remove their coat and open any purses or bags they are carrying. Glenn charges past and up to the maternity ward. The room where he left me earlier today was closest to the entrance of the maternity ward and directly in front of the nursing station, but the picture of peace and serenity he remembers leaving a short while ago has turned on its head. The door to my room is closed and cordoned off with yellow police tape, which he breaks through as the police stationed outside try to hold him back. He kicks in the door only to find the room is empty, save for the team of investigators dusting for fingerprints and shoe impressions. The activity inside the room stops as the investigators look up to see what the commotion is.

Glenn yells, "Where is my wife?"

"You have to calm down," an investigator responds.

Glenn repeats, with quiet rage, "Where is my wife?"

A social worker comes in and takes Glenn by the arm. With her hand gently holding his elbow, she guides him out of the room. "Mr. Walsh, your wife is down the hall. I'll take you to her." A detective follows them out of the room and stands close by. The people on either side of Glenn have a calming effect on him as he follows the social worker, and he sees Mary coming down the hall toward them.

"This is my sister," he says, and he reaches over to pull her along, adding, "She's coming with us." The group takes the few short steps to the area of the hospital where I am now stationed.

| CHAPTER 30 |

I have noticed that there is a distinctive sound to the way that everyone walks, and I listen as people pass by my door. I am told that we are in a ward in the hospital that is no longer used — the rooms along this corridor are empty. Time has moved on without a fracture, but there is a crack in my memory and I have no recollection of how I got here. I wonder what happened to the other mothers who I shared a room with and where they were moved to.

I can hear the lights humming and the sound of my sister breathing beside me. We sit on the edge of the bed and it squeaks as we occasionally shift position.

The police have finally arrived. A solemn detective carrying official-looking documents enters and immediately makes eye contact with me, which he maintains as he approaches the bed, possibly trying to determine whether I had any involvement in my own child's abduction. He has a fair complexion, and his dark hair and matching moustache are tidy and well-trimmed. His shoes are shiny, and underneath his overcoat, which is still damp from the winter weather, he is dressed in business clothes. The wrinkles that have begun to form on his otherwise neat attire are evidence of a long work day.

He bends down to my level as he introduces himself and adds, "I am here to ask you for a formal statement."

He has kind eyes and a soft voice but he remains professional. Each word is clear and precise. I like him right away. He has the good sense not to ask me how I am.

I feel so alone. *Glenn where are you? I need my best friend.*

"Take your time," the detective says. "Even the smallest detail that may seem insignificant now could prove to be helpful later."

And just as if I have conjured him up with my thoughts, Glenn comes crashing into the room like a crazed animal. He asks me no questions, just grabs me in a bone-crushing embrace. No one says a word and there is silence in the room. We hold on to each other for dear life, we are each other's life jackets in this sea of despair. When we finally part, I see tears on his face and on the faces of our sisters. The police in the room have been watching him closely and his reaction to seeing me must have eliminated him as the number one suspect.

He sits beside me and introductions are made. The detective resumes his interview. "Diana, tell me everything you can remember."

I begin to recount to the detective what has happened up to this point, and although I am speaking to the detective, I am looking at Glenn. If he can read my mind the way I think he can, he knows I am really saying, *Do you understand? Please forgive me for handing our child over to a stranger. It wasn't my fault. It all seemed to make sense at the time.*

I tell the detective that early on in my pregnancy there was concern about the low iron levels in my blood; consequently,

Shelby's blood was tested after she was born to ensure her health and well-being. She was found to be jaundiced and was thus monitored very closely since her birth. "The lab technician came into my room and took the blood out of her little foot."

My voice is very low, and the detective leans in closer as he continues to write on a lined pad of paper. The more frantic I feel, the more composed and quiet my replies become. Everyone in the room strains to hear my words. "Shelby cried when the blood was drawn." *And I cried right along with her.* "The next time the nurse came into the room to test her blood, there was still a Band-Aid on her foot from the previous day." *The tears flowed down my cheeks before they even touched her.* "I was upset at the prospect of her having to go through the blood work again, and one of the nurses suggested that I go for a walk down the hall until they were finished." *I can still hear the sound of her crying and I feel like sobbing myself.* "When another nurse came for a third time … it didn't seem strange that they were taking her for more blood work … I thought they were just being thorough." I tell him everything I can remember.

"Can you describe her for me?"

We look at people all the time, but we don't really see them: the grocery clerk, the waitress, the person who pumps our gas or passes a coffee through the drive-through window. I wonder how many people would be able to describe the last stranger they came in contact with.

I search the recesses of my mind for any detail about her that I can remember, and it slowly comes back to me. "She had hair to about here," I say, gesturing to indicate the length, and resume concentrating. "It was a kind of dirty blond, or brown."

There is a long pause as I try to formulate my thoughts. "Her face was very round." *Does that even make sense?* He doesn't stop me to clarify what round means, so I guess it does.

"How tall would you say she was?" *Good question.*

"She wasn't tall." *I was on the bed and went up on my knees when she took the baby from me. Her head came up to about my shoulder so that would make her ...* my mind drifts. *My God, did I actually hand my baby over? From my loving arms to the arms of someone who ...*

I am brought back to the present by the persistent detective. "How tall would you say she was?"

"She wasn't tall ... maybe about five-three or five-two."

"And her figure — was she thin, heavy?"

"She wasn't thin ... she was ... she wasn't thin."

"Was she wearing glasses? Did you notice the colour of her eyes? *Damn.* "I'm not sure."

"Did she have any kind of an accent?"

If this is a test, I'm failing miserably. My fingers are clenched so tightly that I can feel my nails digging into the palms of my hands. "I can't be sure."

"What was she wearing?"

Oh ... I know this one! "She was dressed in a nurse's uniform."

"Did she have a name tag on?"

"I don't remember."

"Did she have any other identifying features that you can think of ... anything at all?"

I shake my head. *Oh God ... what have I done?*

"Diana?"

"No. I can't think of anything."

He continues to ask questions, and when he is finished interrogating, he says, "Read the pages carefully — after you have gone over it, sign it to confirm that it's accurate."

He places paper and pen in my hands and I look down at it. I look up at him, and he hasn't taken his eyes off of me. He nods. It's a gentle encouragement: *You can do it.* I look back down and the writing blurs. I blink and try to read, but seconds stretch into minutes and I seem to be at the same spot where I started. I'm still on the first paragraph.

All I can think of is Shelby, even when I close my eyes; her face is imprinted on the inside of my eyelids. Reading right now is impossible, but I sign the statement he has written and hand it back to him without any changes.

I tell the detective that I have pictures in my camera of the children holding the baby from their visit earlier today and wonder if he can use them, if they will help. He says he will take the camera and have the pictures developed right away, then distribute them to the police and the media for immediate publication.

Glenn and I are both looking out the window. From this vantage point on the third floor, facing the lakeshore, our attention has been drawn to the activity below. People are kicking through the snowbanks. They are searching the ditches and the garbage dumpster that is visible below the window. The visible exhalation of their breath confirms my fear of how cold it is outside: it is below zero, and my baby, slightly bigger than five pounds, is out there somewhere, in the cold, without a coat. Dark, disturbing images assault my mind and I am consumed with unadulterated fear. Thoughts of what could be happening to her are unbearable. I start to go there, and then I pull myself back. "... Detective?"

He looks into my eyes and his face shows no emotion, but I feel his compassion and something else that I can't put my finger on. Maybe sympathy.

"Can you tell me how many cases like this ... I mean babies gone missing ... has your department worked on?" I am hoping this will give me some kind of statistic, an indication of what my chances are.

He hesitates for a moment before he answers, "We've never had a case like this before."

| CHAPTER 31 |

It takes someone special to become a police officer — someone with enough courage to put their life on the line every day to ensure the safety of others they've never even met. It takes a true hero. Police are committed to the law and order of their community and fellow man, even on their days off, through special events and holidays. Officers leave their home, kiss their spouses and children goodbye, and spend inhuman hours trying to crack different cases to bring the perpetrators to justice. Some of them will see unspeakable atrocities and have to live with the visual evidence of evil walking among us.

Sergeant Doug Ford, a man with years of experience and the respect of his peers, has been assigned as lead investigator in the case of missing baby Shelby Walsh. Every available person on shift is assigned to the investigation: officers are pulled from the Christmas Reduced Impaired Driving Everywhere (RIDE) program and off-duty officers have shown up to help in the search. In total, there are over fifty local police officers looking for "Baby Shelby," as she will quickly become known. The Criminal Investigation Bureau and the Major Crimes Unit promptly become involved in the search. A nationwide alert notifies all of Canada of the kidnapping, and as tips are called in to the 911 emergency response lines, Sergeant Doug Ford judges their validity and assigns officers to follow up on information.

Doug Ford, like many of the other officers who are trying to save Shelby, worked on the Green Ribbon Task Force, the operation that investigated the infamous Paul Bernardo and Carla Homolka case. Following the task force's apprehension of these monsters, Bernardo was found guilty of nine charges against him, including rape and murder, and sentenced to life in prison without possibility of parole for twenty-five years. Homolka, his wife, was convicted of manslaughter and sentenced to a mere twelve years. There would never be sufficient justice or punishment for the heinous crimes they committed. How could there be? The families would never again know peace. These officers do not want another colour ribbon to remind them of an unhappy ending.

December 23, 1993
3:30 P.M.

The police bring in and introduce two people from Victim Services. To me they are just more strangers in the room, and I explain to them that although I appreciate their offer of support and help, I have my family here and I would really rather be with them … only them. The Victim Services people leave before they have even had a chance to utter a word.

A social worker is also brought into the room and starts to talk to me about the grieving process and how to deal with loss. I am speechless. Debbie brings her out to the hall and tells her to back off. "There is nothing to grieve about. This is not someone suffering from an incurable disease or someone who has lost a loved one in an open-heart surgery. If you don't have any experience in this area, then maybe you should leave."

My body quakes as my uterus, stretched to the size of a watermelon in pregnancy, attempts to contract its way back to the size of a chestnut. The after pains have increased in intensity in direct proportion to the number of pregnancies I have had. Along with the after pains, nature has also seen fit for me to continue producing milk, even though none has been emptied from my body in hours. My skin has stretched way beyond the point of comfort to accommodate this overload of milk, and I can't relieve the ache. I shift from one position to another, but the milk keeps building and my discomfort increases.

While Debbie is in the hall with the social worker, a nurse approaches and asks if it would be all right to bring me a breast pump to release the milk. The social worker doesn't think it's a good idea: why give false hope that my baby will be coming back? Debbie disagrees. She says the breast pump is needed, but she would rather be the one to bring it to me.

"I want my baby." I'm not speaking to anyone in particular — I'm just thinking out loud. I am quietly keening as I rock back and forth, and my lament is heard and felt by everyone in the room. Debbie enters with a breast pump and sits down beside me. She looks up at me and then down at the pump she has on her lap. "We can save the milk for when Shelby gets back," she says.

She hands the pump to me and looks at me as she waits for a response. I think about it. I really don't want my milk to explode over everyone in the room, but I don't know if I can do it. My head drops down as I ponder, and there is an awkward silence.

I see that I am wearing a yellow maternity shirt that is now baggy over my much flatter stomach. I remember mom saying, "Blondes shouldn't wear yellow." Mom also says that redheads shouldn't wear red, and short people shouldn't wear horizontal stripes. I don't recognize the sweater that I am wearing over my yellow shirt — it is dark blue with coloured flowers — not breaking any of Mom's fashion rules but I'm curious because I don't know where it came from. I don't remember changing out of my nightgown and into my clothing, yet I am wearing stretch pants with a panel in front, which, unfilled with baby, is a droopy pouch like a kangaroo without its joey. With the hope that I am not still wearing slippers, I look down at my feet and am relieved to see shoes.

As uncomfortable as I am, I just can't do it — I feel like it would be admitting defeat. The breast pump is returned to the nurse and traded for a peri bottle to fill with warm water and cotton sanitary supplies. My body is still reeling from the delivery, and I am reminded of the after care that is necessary. I look down at my hands and I want to weep. My eyes fill and then they clear before I have shed a tear. The sadness in the room is tangible. It is as deep and dark as the ocean and bigger than all of us.

Another doctor enters the room and stands in the doorway. I recognize her as the gynecologist who diagnosed and treated my miscarriage last December. She says, in a choked voice, "Mrs. Walsh, I'm so sorry about your baby."

"Thank you. It was good of you to come down and see me," I say.

My responses are polite and succinct, but I'm holding on for dear life. My emotions are barely contained. I can't afford to let anyone's kindness penetrate the wall I've put up. When the doctor turns to leave, I can see she is trying not to cry. I hear someone saying, "She's in shock." I don't think I'm in shock, but apparently my behaviour is shocking.

"Diana, would you like a little something to relax you?" The nurse who has asked the question is well-meaning. Perhaps she believes drugs will numb the pain, but pain seems fitting at a time like this and I want a clear head. I want to be lucid when any news comes in.

"No, thank you."

I am being polite to everyone because that's the way I was raised, and because it's keeping me from going crazy. If I let myself cross over to the dark place of this new reality, I feel like I may never come back. Outwardly, and to all appearances, I am calm, likely too calm for people to understand, but inwardly I am screaming so loud it is deafening.

I want to find my daughter!

| CHAPTER 32 |

How many people have lingered in a hospital, waiting, praying, and hoping for a miracle as they anticipated news of their loved one? I can only imagine what this old hospital has seen and wonder what stories these walls could tell. There must have been hundreds of tears shed in pain and in great happiness, many shouts of grief and cries of gladness.

Many feet have traversed these halls, but I recognize the footsteps I hear now as belonging to the detective who interviewed me about an hour ago. On alert, I am watching the empty doorway, and my eyes are on him the second he comes into sight. He walks into the room and directly to me, and for a few moments we are still and quiet. I can tell he has something to say, and I want to ask him flat out what it is, but something in his expression stops me — I haven't decided yet if it will be good news or bad. The longer he fidgets, the longer I go without breathing.

The detective looks at me, and I can see the tension in his furrowed brow and taut body. "We have reviewed the security tapes. The camera at the entrance to the hospital shows a woman who matches the description you gave. She had a baby in her arms. The timing of her departure gives us good reason to believe it's her."

"That's good, right? That could be helpful." But my internal voice is saying, *Are you trying to scare the shit out of me? I could have had a heart attack!*

"Yes, it's definitely helpful. The video validates your description of her and we'll be able to get the image out there for people to see."

Uncontrollable, angry words suddenly escape from my mouth: "The next time you have news for me, please cut to the chase and tell it to me quickly." Regret follows in short order as I look up at the detective apologetically. *I'm sorry ... I know it's not your fault.*

The thought of this woman holding my baby makes me queasy: she has my child and she has left the hospital. Who is she? Where has she gone? What is she planning to do?

The detective looks over his shoulder at the sound of more footsteps down the broad corridor — the rest of my family is making their way through the hospital.

When my physician was notified of the kidnapping, she telephoned my mother at work, who immediately called my siblings. It will be years before I learn how everyone reacted to the news.

Maureen was home with her three-year-old son and baby daughter when, in the midst of Christmas preparations, she lifted the telephone receiver to hear Mom say, "Maureen, are you sitting down?"

I now see Maureen and her husband, Mark, walk into the room. I go to my sister's arms; Glenn goes to Mark's arms. There is a circle of weeping.

Elaine appears right behind Maureen.

When Elaine received the call from my mother, she didn't believe that Shelby had been kidnapped. She telephoned the hospital, and they would not put her call through, nor would they confirm or deny any information. My sister then telephoned her husband, who worked for the Toronto police, to see what he could find out. He called back minutes later and confirmed the news: "The Toronto Division has been notified of the kidnapping. They're reporting that Shelby was abducted from the hospital. The border crossings have been notified and there is a province-wide police alert. The police believe that with every minute that passes the chances of finding Shelby grow slimmer. Many scenarios are being considered, including abduction of the baby for sale on the black market." Her husband's last comment took away all hope: "I'm sorry, Elaine, but they are never going to see that baby again."

He is now her ex-husband. I never did like that guy.

My brother, Chuck, shows up next. This boy who grew up without the guidance of a father has become a wonderful husband and a father to four children of his own, and in his eyes I can see his incredulousness at the situation.

Our club is intact. Mom, having contacted everyone, arrives close on their heels. The matriarch is in place and the troops are all here. We band together now for comfort and courage.

Maureen and I are sitting on the bed, inches apart, and she unconsciously starts cracking her knuckles one by one. Glenn and Mark are looking out the window, standing motionless, deep in thought with unspoken fear. The other sisters are leaning against the wall, and occasionally their heads bend in close to one another. Mom doesn't seem to know what to do as she sits down in the straight-backed chair beside the bed and puts her hands in her lap. They say women average seven thousand words a day and men manage a mere two thousand, but right now everyone is speechless in this unused wing of the hospital.

I feel like I have stumbled into a bottomless well, falling and falling, with no idea when I am going to crash. I am so frightened that I feel physically ill.

We are waiting, but for what we don't know.

Chuck has wandered out into the hall. With my hands at my sides, I push down on the bed and slowly raise myself from a sitting position to stand and follow him out. I don't look behind me, but I'm sure that all eyes follow my exit.

Chuck has entered one of the empty rooms across the hall. I overhear him speaking to his wife, Beverly, on the phone: "I think she's in shock …" He stops and turns to face me as I enter the room. His forehead is creased as he slips his free hand under his glasses to rub his eyes in a familiar way. "… Okay … I'll call you later."

"My God, Chuck, can you believe this is happening?"

He shakes his head.

"I don't know if we should stay here, go out and help look for her … I don't know what to do." I look in his eyes and wait for the answer he can't give me. We stand in silence for a while before he puts his arm around my back protectively, then we walk back to join the rest of the family, where we wait for news that doesn't come.

No one knows where my baby is, where my siblings' niece is, or where my mom's grandchild is.

| Chapter 33 |

There is a fine line between madness and sanity, and I am walking it.

We can't stay at the hospital. I don't want to leave. This is the only place my baby knows. If I leave she won't know where to find me. The hospital staff gently tell me that I should go home and relax. "Try to get some rest."

If I didn't think they'd put me in a straight jacket, I might laugh out loud.

By now there's a media circus outside, and the police tell us that most of the exits have a photographer hoping to snap a photo or an interviewer waiting to catch a story.

I feel like I've aged exponentially in the last few hours; I wouldn't be surprised to look in a mirror and find that my hair has gone white. While walking like someone three times my age, I let myself be herded this way and that by a police officer and a hospital staff member. I don't know where I'm going, I haven't asked — I just keep on walking and putting one foot in front of the other.

Glenn and I are led to a damp, cold, dimly lit area beneath the hospital, where my brother-in-law Mark is waiting with his van running. I didn't know there was an underground area. I wonder how he knew about this place and who told him to come here to pick us up. Mark gets out of the van to open the sliding door, and I feel the warmer temperature in the vehicle as Glenn helps me inside. With a loud *thunk*, the police officer slides the door back into place. My eyes rest on the people who walked us out of the hospital, standing side by side, watching us slowly depart.

I am being snuck out — it feels like we're executing a jail break. *Who's the criminal here? Maybe I should talk to the reporters. Maybe I should beg the kidnapper to bring my baby back. I'll make her a false promise that I won't press charges if only she'll bring my baby back safely. I won't tell her I am going to wring her neck with my bare hands.* I am so angry — angry at her, at myself, at the situation.

I am so tormented. *Where is she?* A lot of time has passed, and every hour makes the situation more serious. I am so troubled. *What are the kidnapper's intentions?* Does she want a baby to love as her own, or worse, does she have some sick desire to harm a baby? I remember a conversation I recently overhead between two people who were discussing a shocking news article. The story outlined how criminals were apprehended at the airport after trying to smuggle drugs out of the country — the drugs were hidden inside of a dead baby. The two people having the conversation were questioning whether the baby was murdered for the purpose of smuggling the cocaine or if the child had perished due to natural causes and then was sliced down the middle and stuffed like a thanksgiving turkey.

Scared and confused, I speak to no one. While at the hospital, I held on to the hope that at some point someone was going to walk around the corner with Shelby and tell me it was all some terrible mistake. I can't believe it. It is not a mistake. I am going home without my baby. As I wrap my arms around myself, I realize I am still wearing the sweater that doesn't belong to me. Sadly, I think, it's a very nice sweater; someone is going to miss it.

While we drive down the street, I am looking outside. The only light comes from the streetlights we occasionally pass. My eyes dart back and forth, looking for the Shadow of a baby girl, and I know that for the rest of my life, I will be looking out of windows at every little girl I see. Now I am looking for an infant, but in a few years I will be looking for a little girl, and I will be trying to see if it is *my* little girl. Are her eyes brown? Does she have cornsilk hair? Does she have a freckle between the two smallest toes on her right foot? "Excuse me, little girl. Would you mind taking off your right shoe so I can examine your foot?"

I realize my daughter will someday be seen in posters at the mall and on the back of transport trucks in an age-enhanced photograph. HAVE YOU SEEN THIS CHILD? MISSING SINCE DECEMBER 1993.

My misery is so great that it hurts to breathe. I think about the many parents who are suffering over their missing children, and now I am one of them. I think of the Dunahee family in British Columbia, whose son Michael went missing in 1991. I have thought of them often over the years. When the news broke that their son had been kidnapped, I could relate to their family. Michael Dunahee was the same age as my son when he was kidnapped, and he had the same name. He had a sister named Caitlin, the same name as our daughter, and was close to her age.

Michael Dunahee went to the playground with his parents, and they let him out of their sight just briefly as they went around the corner to get his little sister. Minutes later, when they got back to the playground, he had disappeared. He was four years old and has never been seen again. They have never found even one shred of evidence as to his whereabouts. He seemed to vanish into thin air.

His room remains the same since he went missing: his clothes still in the drawers, toys still on his bed, and posters still on the walls. Every year at Christmas, they buy a special present for him and add it to the pile of gifts on his shelf, waiting for his return. I wonder what happened to that little boy. I wonder if his mother is feeling as I am now.

Someone knows what happened to that boy, and someone out there knows what happened to Shelby. Someone is tormenting the Dunahee family each day that their child continues to be missing. Although I have thought of them often, I never thought I'd be in their position or feel the same anguish.

My child is missing.

*Missing ... what kind of a word is missing? There has to be a stronger word to portray what has happened to these children. I have a sock box at home with a bunch of socks that have no mate. Those are "missing." Children are not missing, they are ... kidnapped, they are stolen, they are abducted, they are **not** missing!*

Glenn breaks the silence when he says to me, "We had three children and now we have two ... we have to be strong for them. We will survive this, and we will make a good life for ourselves. We love each other and we will get through this."

I can't swallow; there is a lump in my throat that is the size of a plum. Things will never be the same again — for me, for him, for my family. In an instant everything has changed. The sadness in the vehicle is palpable. The tears want to come, but my eyes are dry. It hurts too much to cry. I continue to stare out of the window, lost in a never-ending assault of thoughts, recriminations, and second guesses:

> *If I'd left the hospital an hour earlier this wouldn't have happened ... but I didn't.*
> *If I'd said I wanted to go with her when she went for blood work ... but I didn't.*
> *If I'd gone out to the hall when I thought I heard a baby's cry ... but I didn't.*
> *When ifs and buts are candies and nuts we'll all have a wonderful Christmas.*

Grandma holding Shelby.

Michael and Caitlin holding their sister during the hospital visit on the day she was kidnapped.

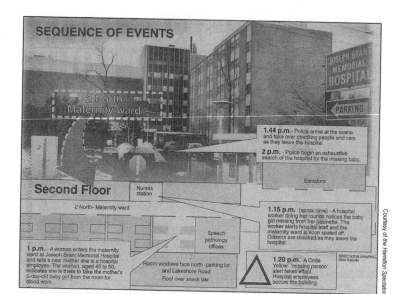

SEQUENCE OF EVENTS

2 North Maternity ward

1.44 p.m. - Police arrive at the scene and take over checking people and cars as they leave the hospital.

2 p.m. - Police begin an exhaustive search of the hospital for the missing baby.

Elevators

Second Floor
Nurses station

2 North- Maternity ward

Speech pathology offices

1.15 p.m. (aprox. time) - A hospital worker doing her rounds notices the baby girl missing from her basinette. The worker alerts hospital staff and the maternity ward is soon sealed off. Citizens are checked as they leave the hospital.

1 p.m. - A woman enters the maternity ward at Joseph Brant Memorial Hospital and tells a new mother she is a hospital employee. The woman, aged 45 to 50, indicates she is there to take the mother's 5-day-old baby girl from the room for blood work.

Room windows face north parking lot and Lakeshore Road
Roof over snack bar

1.20 p.m. A Code Yellow 'missing person' alert takes effect. Hospital employees secure the building.

SPECTATOR GRAPHIC, Mike Batista

Top: The sequence of events. Note that the timeline shown was estimated. The actual 911 call was placed at 12:54, and the lockdown occurred at 12:54:47.

Right: A Halton police officer searching cars leaving the hospital.

| CHAPTER 34 |

I often wonder about the power of prayer, whether the combined energy of thousands of focused thoughts can truly influence the outcome of an event. Grandma Walsh is from Fermeuse, a small town in Newfoundland, and she believes; earlier today she started a prayer train. Over the last few hours, it has continued to escalate. She first phoned her family in Newfoundland, starting with her sister-in-law Tish: "Tish, is it true what you have told me ... that all of your prayers are always answered?"

Tish answers in her thick Newfoundland brogue, "Yis girl, whattis it you need?"

"Glenn and Diana's baby has been kidnapped. Please, Tish, say a prayer for them."

"NO! Jaysus, Mary, and Joseph."

Tish calls the rest of the family, delivering variations of "Shelby's been kidnapped, and Patricia needs our prayers." When she has finished her calls, she gets down on her knees and begins moving her fingers along her rosary beads.

"In the name of the Father, and Son, and of the Holy Spirit, amen," she says as her right hand swiftly moves from her forehead to her breastbone to her left and right shoulder. "I believe in God, the Father Almighty, Creator of heaven and earth. And in Jesus Christ, His only Son, our Lord, Who was conceived by the Holy Spirit …" She continues through all eighty-one beads, reciting the words she knows by heart.

When she stands she does not stop praying. She continues her plea as she puts a log of wood in her stove, as she dresses for the cold, and as she drives down the lane to pick up her sister Mary, who she told, "Stay where you're to and I'll come where you're at."

The sisters go to their local church and ask the priest to pray for the safe return of Shelby. He delivers a passionate sermon that unites the assembled group, and the heart of the parishioners beat in harmony. They put the well-being of a little girl, a child they have never met, ahead of their own troubles.

When the priest leads the congregation in prayer, there is a common petition: return this child safely to her family. Hope is in the air; it hums down the aisles and passes from one person to the next, embraced and nurtured by everyone in the crowded room. The devotion is a living, breathing thing, and as it is fed, it grows.

Grandma Walsh calls her three sons who live in British Columbia. They can't believe what has happened, and they follow the newscasts from afar. As children they attended church every Sunday, as adults they have not, but they pray for the safe return of their niece, and included in their prayers are promises of their renewed faith.

Grandma Walsh calls her prayer partners in our town. They reach out and call their friends, who in turn phone their friends.

Many of them bring the news to their own parishes and the pleas grow exponentially. The dominos are in motion. From the eastern shores of Newfoundland to the west coast of British Columbia, there are multitudes praying for us.

My cousin living in the Dominican Republic sees the newscast on CNN and joins in the prayers, as do many others around the world, as the story is now being followed globally. A baby has been kidnapped two days before Christmas, and the world community is outraged and intrigued.

As the nation joins in the prayer train, many letters are sent to the hospital and forwarded to me at home in the days that follow.

> I have four children. Two were born in December. There is an extra special excitement when babies are born at Christmas time. When I heard what had happened with baby Shelby, my heart broke. I started to pray. I prayed all day and all evening. When I got up with my babies, I pleaded with God to have this lady caught. I prayed to my lord for your baby's safety. I prayed so hard my heart ached and my eyes shed many, many tears.
> Sheila W., Ontario

> I am a complete stranger — you might well be leery of strangers at this point, but I just had to send a small note. On the day that you lost your little one, I was driving to town to get groceries — it was 8:00 at night and I was very tired but when I heard on the radio your baby was taken. I was overwhelmed with sorrow. I can't go buy a poster of a missing child without feeling great sorrow. I prayed and I wept. I cried out in the name of love and compassion to return your little

one, that the kidnapper would be recognized and that people would be alert and look for her.
Fiona W., Nova Scotia

You don't know me. I am writing to tell you how sorry I am about the kidnapping of your baby. While I was preparing dinner I heard the news bulletin on CNN. I mourned for your great loss and prayed for her safe return. I spoke to my friends and they were praying also. I would have given away everything under my Christmas tree if only you would get your baby back.
Rebecca S., Saskatchewan

Arlene and I heard your news with such sympathy, our hearts are with you.
Bob Rae, Premier of Ontario

There is something about the loss of a child that everyone takes to heart. We see a lot of suffering in the world, but when it involves a child, it touches us all the more and we tolerate it all the less.

| CHAPTER 35 |

December 23, 1993
2:45 P.M.

The kidnapper calls a taxi to pick her up from her basement apartment. With her baby sleeping inside of a knapsack between her feet, the kidnapper instructs the driver to take her to the Big V at 484 Plains Road East in Burlington. She stares silently out the window as they drive.

As she enters the pharmacy, which is filled with last-minute Christmas shoppers, she struggles with the knapsack while she loosens her winter coat. The kidnapper heads for the sign BABY CARE hanging above aisle four. She passes a variety of shampoos, soaps, baby wipes, and creams, then picks up a bottle of baby oil and keeps on walking. Next, she comes upon the diaper section. She is baffled by the multitude of styles of diapers: "Day wear," "Night wear," "Pull ups," "Pin ups," and "Tape ups." There is also the option of unscented or scented — one package even boasts the fragrance of cucumbers. In the end, she makes her selection based on size: a small package will be easy for her to carry. She moves on, to look for something to feed the baby.

Stacks of baby food jars and boxed cereal overwhelm her. She walks past all of these and stops in front of the formula, wondering when the choices became so complicated. The options of soya, omega-3, omega-6, hypoallergenic, and iron-fortified are bewildering. Other shoppers are focused on their own purchases, and the strange woman wandering around in confusion through the baby section goes unnoticed. Starting to feel uncomfortable with all of these decisions, the kidnapper reaches past the powder formula mix and chooses a liquid brand in a can. She indiscriminately chooses formula for a six-month-old baby.

From the large selection of baby bottles, she opts for one that requires sterilization before every use. Disposable bags to be used as bottle liners seem like an awful waste of money and completely unnecessary.

As the Shadow is paying for her purchases, the cashier happens to notice the baby and innocently inquires, "How old is your baby?" The Shadow covers the child's face with a blanket and replies, "He is three months old," referring to the baby as a boy.

| Chapter 36 |

December 23, 1993
3:45 P.M.

An hour after the kidnapper leaves the Big V, Lori, a staff member from the hospital, stops at the store to pick up a few things on her way home from work. She has a conversation with the cashiers. "Have you heard about what happened at the hospital?"

"No, what's going on?"

"There was a baby kidnapped from maternity." Noticeably upset, Lori tells the cashiers about the situation at the hospital, and this leaves a lasting impression on the cashiers.

As Lori walks through the store to make her purchases, the cashiers continue to discuss the kidnapping, when Judi Good and Kathy Langdon remember the woman who was in earlier to purchase formula. For the moment, business is slow, and they have a few minutes to talk. As they speak they look over their shoulders to ensure that the manager is not watching. They have both been warned that there are secret shoppers in the store that are not shoppers at all but corporate personnel. They never know who may be evaluating their performance, and they don't want to be seen as gossips. Judi says, "That woman who was in here not that long ago ... She was kind of strange looking and she had a baby."

"She wasn't really dressed for the winter weather and neither was her baby," Kathy responds in a low voice, trying to remain discreet.

"And she was carrying that baby around in a knapsack that kids use to carry their books to school in. What mother does that?"

Kathy nods, adding, "The formula she purchased was for a six-month-old and her baby looked much younger."

"She told me he was three months old, but he was very tiny for three months."

"Did she say her baby was a boy?"

"She did ... Well, she said *he* was three months old, but who can tell at that age."

Some new customers approach the check-out counter and the conversation abruptly stops.

| CHAPTER 37 |

We are home. I barely notice the change in temperature from the warm van to the cold outdoors — I am numb. The frigid weather appears to respect our despair and need for silence, as there is not even a breath of wind to be heard. The only sound is that of snow crunching underfoot as Glenn and I walk down the driveway toward the front door and the task that looms before us. Mark is following close behind us.

The house is well-lit, and to an unknowing observer would look warm and inviting. I can see the lights from the Christmas tree shining through the living room window and a few silhouettes of people through the sheer curtains.

When we enter the house, my father-in-law opens his arms. As he embraces us, I feel the quiver of his body. He is weeping.

His seven children have never witnessed his tears. We shift to the arms of other family members, who also give comfort and share in our grief. While being held by my brother-in-law Wayne, I see my father-in-law bow his head and leave the room. I follow his lead and remove myself from the crowd.

My family watches me walk down the hall to the freshly decorated nursery. No one follows me, and I hear their hushed conversations behind me. The room unfolds before me. The walls are painted a shade of sky blue and match the small rug, which covers the hardwood floor. The white blinds with tassels are pulled shut beneath lace curtains on the window. The beautiful maple crib, a gift from a brother and sister, is empty except for the blankets and protective white eyelet bumper pad. I remember when Glenn's dad assembled the crib. He came out of the nursery, handed me a bunch of nuts and bolts from the assembly kit, and said, "I didn't need these."

There is a colourful wallpaper border just above the baseboards. I have seen other borders pasted midway on walls, but this border is a collage of stuffed animals, and I liked the look of them all sitting on the floor. Now, dozens of teddy bear eyes are on me as I approach the white change table — a treasure found and rescued by Glenn's father, Patrick, before it was taken away and discarded as garbage.

The creams and powders line the change table beside the baby facecloths. The diapers are lined up, and the little undershirts I took such care in organizing remain folded and ready to go. Dozens of receiving blankets, well-worn with the softness that only comes after hundreds of washings, line the bottom shelf. The room smells lightly of the baby fabric softener that was used in the laundry.

Rarely have I seen such order and symmetry in my house, and although I have always envied such organization in others, it now saddens me. Glass chimes of pink ballerina slippers and yellow balloons hang in the corner, where Glenn placed them earlier in the month. They slowly tinkle when I pass.

Grandma Walsh is standing over the empty crib with her rosary.

She has had to say goodbye to her sister Mary this week. Although I could not attend Mary's funeral in Newfoundland, I took heart in the fact that Shelby's soul had entered this world just as Mary's was gently leaving. While I grieved for the loss of Mary, I also smiled at the thought that she would be able to keep an eye on Shelby from afar — her own personal guardian angel. I pray she is watching over her now. Grandma Walsh is also quietly praying. Her faith is unwavering. "They will find her, Diana."

"From your lips to God's ears."

| CHAPTER 38 |

We have decided to tell the children what has happened right away, before they hear something on the television or radio. It will be difficult for them to understand, but it will be even more terrifying if they hear it from someone they don't know, and by now the story is big news. The details of the kidnapping are being broadcast on all of the local stations and continue to be the tag line on the bottom of the screen for CNN.

Our son is seven years old, and our daughter is five.

Glenn and I go into the family room, and the children, playing with their Aunt Elaine, have not noticed us enter. There are few precious moments when I am able to watch them before they see me, and I savour their beauty and innocence. I note they have their Treasure Trolls among their toys, proudly displaying their status as big brother and big sister.

A movement catches their eye, and they look up to see me. Big smiles appear like the sun on a cloudy day, and excitement shows not only in their faces but also in the squeals of delight that peal through the room as they run in my direction. "You're home! Where is the baby?"

We have read them books on proper safety. One has the painting of a scary man hiding something sinister looking behind his back. We turn the page to see that the dark object he is holding is actually an umbrella, and the scary looking man is a kind person who helps his neighbour come in out of the rain. Further in the story we see a smiling, cheerful man who is also holding something behind his back. We turn the page to see that it's a club, and the person is actually mean and dangerous — reaffirming the age-old lesson that a wolf may be unrecognizable when it's in sheep's clothing. We have had the talks with them about strangers. You never ever, ever, under any circumstances speak to strangers. We have given them different scenarios to consider. "If a stranger comes up to you at school and says Mommy and Daddy have sent them to give you a ride home, what do you do?"

"We don't talk to them. We run into the school and tell the teacher." They look at us to confirm they have given the correct answer.

"If someone came into our yard and said they wanted you to help them look for their doggy, what would you do?"

They smile as they answer, "We don't talk to them — we run into the house right away and tell you."

We'd done a great job! We continued, "If a stranger approaches you and asks you if you want a candy, what do you do?"

They repeat, in unison, "I say yes please."

Back to square one.

They have been instructed in every situation we could possibly think of and trained repeatedly on personal safety. And yet, here I am, about to tell them that their little sister was taken away by a stranger — that some strangers are so sly that they can even trick grownups.

I take a deep breath and say, quietly, "She's not here." Glenn and I sit down and gather them between us. "Something kinda scary happened today." I look at Glenn and he nods in agreement, then I look back at the children. I see them look at their father before their curious eyes settle back on mine.

I have been fooled by a wolf in sheep's clothing. How can I explain something I don't understand myself? Do I say that sociopaths are good at fooling people — that they know how to read people and say the right thing? You are not suspicious of their wrongdoing because you could never conceive of doing it yourself. They would likely respond, "What's a sociopath, Mommy?"

Instead, I say, "A lady came into the hospital today. She didn't have a baby of her own and she wanted one very badly. She saw our baby ..." I take a deep breath, and compose myself. "... And she took it home, even though it didn't belong to her."

They have not said a word. Their little minds process this new piece of information.

"Now, we're not sure where she lives, so everyone is out looking for the lady so they can bring the baby back home to us. The doctors and nurses are looking for her, all our friends and neighbours are looking for her, and even the policemen are looking for her." I want to cry, but don't let myself, because I'm afraid they will see how scared I am.

Caitlin looks at me with sad eyes and says, "I wanted that baby very badly." Her little chin trembles.

The simplicity and honesty of a child is a beautiful thing. I gather her in my arms with a burning love. "I know you did, honey."

With her head burrowed against my chest, she then says, in a voice now turning angry, "Santa is going to bring that bad lady a lump of coal."

My son, who seems wise beyond his years, asks, "Will they find the baby, Mama?"

"I hope so, honey."

| CHAPTER 39 |

Our siblings are with us, and as the aunts and uncles take turns distracting the children, we gather around the television. We are listening for any bit of information that may give us some answers. We have the channel turned to the local station, CHCH news. The broadcaster reads from his teleprompter: "Tonight, police officers were going door to door in apartment buildings north of the hospital looking for witnesses or any clues on the disappearance of a baby girl."

We see a clip of officers knocking on a door. When no one answers, they kneel down and yell through a mail slot. The door opens and an unidentified person is questioned.

Now, Sergeant Joe Martin, from media relations in the police department, is on the screen: "A woman came in dressed in what appeared to be a nurse's uniform ... a hospital smock. She had a brief conversation with two other women who had their children in the room. A short time after being there, she spoke to the child's mother and told her that she had to take her baby downstairs for some blood work. Some twenty minutes later, it was determined that the child had been abducted. Police began searching everyone leaving the hospital."

There is a clip of the exit at the hospital, and police stopping everyone trying to leave, opening coats and checking in purses. Voiced over this is a newscaster, saying, "Baby Shelby is five days old and weighs less than six pounds. She may have been wrapped in a multicoloured green, pink, and blue blanket."

I think over this comment about the colourful blanket and try to travel back in time in the recesses of my memory to see if there is anything there to suggest a colourful blanket. I do have a blurry vision of a colourful blanket, and this gives me the creeps. *Where did I see that blanket? Was it under the bassinet?*

As the clip changes to the parking lot of the hospital and cars stopped with their trunks open, being searched, the newscaster continues, "The suspect is forty to fifty years of age, about five-foot-three, stocky build with short, slightly curly hair and a round face. She may have worn a three-quarter-length green and blue coat."

All of the suspect's characteristics are displayed in bold lettering. "If the woman that took this child today is watching, please reconsider what you have done and bring the child back." The sergeant is visibly moved as he continues, "Bring her somewhere ... to the hospital ... to the police. As you might be aware, this is obviously more than a nightmare for the parents of this child." He looks directly in to the camera. "The mother is extremely distraught, as is the father and the rest of the family. They're ... uh ... I think I could describe it as ... they're in shock."

We now hear a closing comment from the newscaster. "Police are reviewing video from hospital surveillance cameras tonight."

Glenn and I are cuddled together, facing the television in a large cream-coloured armchair that is meant for one person. Our family is on the other side of the room, also facing the television.

I lean in close to him and whisper, "Even though I am exhausted and I don't think there is an inch of me that doesn't hurt right now, I think I would like to make love." I think it would be comforting to be that close to each other right now. He has been by my side through so many of life's hurdles, and he is the only one that hurts like I do right now, from the inside out. Glenn looks at me like I have a few screws loose and makes a comment that leaves no doubt of the impossibility of my suggestion. We share a laugh, and I catch my sister's eye from across the room. She is regarding me quizzically, and her quiet response is the now-familiar phrase, "She's in shock."

I think, with amused despair, that during times of great peril, it is still possible to laugh.

I suppose my laughter seems inappropriate to an onlooker, but is there a correct response at a time like this? Emily Post didn't cover this in her manual on proper etiquette: "Chapter thirteen, what to do when your child is kidnapped: thank you notes that should be written, clothes that should be worn." I wonder if people would think it more suitable for me to be curled up in a corner, crying. Maybe I should do something crazy like run through the neighbourhood howling like a wolf. I would like to throw tomatoes at passing cars, slap a total stranger across the face so hard it leaves a red mark, throw a lamp through the front picture window, or smash the cars outside with a baseball bat. I have been traumatized, but I am still me. For now, I will only fantasize about doing these things. For today, this is how I deal with catastrophe.

The newscaster starts a new broadcast, and we see a hospital representative who gives a brief statement. "A baby disappeared from the maternity wing of the hospital sometime between one and one fifteen this afternoon. Shortly before then, witnesses told police they saw a middle-aged woman in the wing posing as a lab technician.

"She indicated she was taking a baby from a room for blood work. She took the child and it is believed that she now left the hospital. A very short time later, a hospital staff doing her rounds noticed the baby missing from a bassinet, made some inquiries, and immediately alerted the police and the hospital that the child was missing. The hospital was put on a code yellow — a warning of a missing patient. Officers searched bags and coats at all entrances for clues of the missing baby. Drivers leaving the parking lot had to open their trunks for inspection. Inspectors continue their search for a suspect."

Once again the description is shown in bold letters on the screen:

WHITE FEMALE

45-50 YEARS

SHORT (STOUT)

AQUA HOSPITAL VOLUNTEER SMOCK

I think back to the kidnapper and try to remember if she was wearing an aqua smock, but I can't picture it. I know she had hospital clothes on, but for the life of me I can't remember what colour they were, and this disturbs me. I wonder where they got this piece of information about the aqua smock and if there is anything else the police are not telling me.

The camera once again pans to people and cars being inspected.

Once again, we hear Sergeant Joe Martin as he closes the broadcast: "It's a nightmare." He shakes his head. "A nightmare before Christmas."

And so it goes for the entire evening. Our family, including mothers, brothers, sisters, and their spouses, who have since joined the group, all gathered in the living room, watching and listening to the news bulletins as they come in.

| CHAPTER 40 |

From my vantage point in the armchair, I see an oil painting. The colours are muted, shades of yellow and rust. As our taste in decor has always been very different, it's one of the few pieces of art that Glenn and I both agreed on liking. The painting depicts a mother with a Mona-Lisa-type smile leaning over a child in a cradle, which is blanketed by an antique quilt. The child is looking up at the mother in recognition, in wonder. I rub my eyes as the image now blurs.

On the opposite wall are two black and white photographs I took of Michael and Caitlin. Michael, at the age of three, is peaking out behind a tree, and Caitlin, not yet one year old, is trying to look over a wooden picket fence on her tippy toes. She is wearing a cotton summer dress decorated with lace and frills. The children look so carefree and happy with their big smiles and their hair blowing in the wind. I wonder if anyone in my family will ever be carefree again, and when I see their troubled faces across the room, I have to look away.

I glance down and my eyes clear as I focus my attention on the old Timex wristwatch on my left arm, purchased with the promise that "it takes a licking but keeps on ticking." The watch has been my trusted companion for over twenty years. Earlier in the week, I used it to monitor my contractions. That seems like such a long time ago.

I am comforted by the white face, which has turned beige over the years. I like the discoloration brought on by time. It's something ordinary that I can cling to. My right hand rubs the familiar, well-worn brown leather band. I see the gold second hand crawl over the black numbers in slow motion, and I hear it tick.

Time is funny stuff; our perception of it is ever-changing. Minutes feel like seconds to the parents saying goodbye to their enlisted child. Those same minutes can feel like hours when waiting to hear of the soldier's safe return.

Not even a full minute has passed since I last checked the time. Visions of a baby girl being tortured circle my mind.

My mind continues to drift, and new horrors keep trying to enter the realm of possibility. They sicken me. I try to banish the unwelcome thoughts, but they swarm like bees. They are relentless and keep coming back to sting me.

There are Christmas cards on the mantel and five homemade knitted stockings hanging below them. Tomorrow, Santa will come to fill them. What will he do about Shelby's stocking?

No one has thought to light a fire, but it is just a passing thought and I don't suggest that anyone make the effort now. The heat of the flames could not bring the warmth that my body craves.

The Christmas tree we cut down at the tree farm stands in the corner, several brightly wrapped gifts tucked beneath it. On the floor lies a broken glass ornament that no one has bothered to pick up. The carpet needs vacuuming, and a comic book lies open under the dining room table.

Several muted conversations are going on throughout the room. It is unusually quiet. Typically, when my family is together you can't hear yourself think for the sound of loud music, conversations, and generous laughter. Plenty of banging and crashing can always be heard in the kitchen as food is prepared and drinks are served, but my hostess duties have fallen by the wayside. I have not asked anyone if they would like a drink, and it's probable that no one has eaten today. But, again, it is just a passing thought, and I do nothing to rectify the situation.

As the doorbell rings, all heads turn, and Glenn and I jump up to find my neighbour has had the foresight to bring a tray of snacks over for us, from her preparations for tomorrow's annual Christmas Eve gala. Glenn takes the tray to the dining room table while I stay at the door.

This neighbour and friend was my walking companion during a time when we were both expecting. As many women can attest to, many stories are shared while walking with a friend and topics are discussed that would normally be kept confidential. I remember a story of when my friend had one of her children by Caesarean section that truly exemplifies how vulnerable we are after giving birth. Her abdominal muscles were so tender from being invaded by the surgeon that she could barely walk down the hall the following day. After she finally arrived at her destination, the shower, she looked with trepidation at the two inches she was going to have to lift her foot to enter the stall, then she saw a nurse coming her way. She called the woman over and asked for her assistance. Holding the good Samaritan's arm for balance, my neighbour removed her robe and handed it over. After she made it gingerly over the few inches that seemed like a few yards, her helper responded, "Are you okay now?"

"Yes, I'm fine. Thank you for your help."

"Do you want me to get you a nurse now?"

Aghast, the new mother realized she had asked some unsuspecting visitor to help her into the shower.

Not only is my neighbour a confidante, but she has recently had a child and is full of compassion for our plight. We continue talking, but neither of us can voice what is really on our mind.

"I thought you might be hungry...."

"Thank you for bringing the tray over...."

If I were a comic book character, like the ones in the book under the dining room table, the bubble above my head would show a different conversation: "I am so sad. I hurt beyond measure. I feel the pain of a hundred blades being scraped across my skin."

After my neighbour leaves, no one else comes to the door. The phone doesn't ring.

A cold sensation alerts me that my shirt is wet — an unpleasant reminder that I have not fed my baby. Debbie catches me looking down at my now stained shirt and brings me down the hall, then produces some fabric out of nowhere and proceeds to bind me as tight as a drum. Now I know how those poor women felt in the 1800s when they were squeezed into corsets. This is one of the saddest moments of my life: I am wondering if my baby is being fed. Is she dry? Is she warm on this cold night? How could this have happened? I want to scream and yell, but I won't. My other two children are down the hall.

I begin to hum a song about a cold winter's day — about a December that is dark — about feeling very, very alone.

I say to no one in particular, "Simon and Garfunkel, 'Sounds of Silence,' I don't know what comes next."

| CHAPTER 41 |

December 23, 1993
4:00 P.M.

The kidnapper has walked from the Big V to the Town & Country Motel at 517 Plains Road East in Burlington. The motel is a one-storey beige-brick structure with faded cream-coloured siding, in obvious need of repair. A big red and yellow sign, LARGE CLEAN ROOMS AND A FRIENDLY ATMOSPHERE! can be seen from the roadside, however, on the door to the registration office, two warnings read ABSOLUTELY NO REFUNDS and $10 PER HOUR CHARGE FOR STAYING BEYOND 11:00 A.M.

A bead of sweat trickles down her forehead. This is caused not by anxiety, as she feels no guilt or remorse, but rather from the physical stress of carrying the baby in her knapsack along with the heavy bags from the store. She leaves both on the ground outside of the office door before entering the reception area. When the door opens, a bell rings.

The kidnapper gives a phoney name and address. After paying thirty-eight dollars in cash, she leaves the front office, picks up her belongings, and walks across the empty parking lot. There are twenty even numbers on one side of the parking lot and twenty odd numbers on the other. She turns a metal key in the doorknob of number 14, a room she has stayed in before. Violent fights have driven her from the basement apartment she shares with her common-law husband and brought her to this motel on more than one occasion.

A musty smell greets her as she enters the room. The corner of the base heater is broken, and it crackles in a feeble attempt to produce heat. Lumps of dust and stray hairs stick out of the shoddily painted baseboards. No one has bothered to repair the scrapes and markings on the formerly white walls or fix the chips in the grey tiled floor. The landscape painting on the wall is just as she remembers it, but it has since been joined by a picture of a ship that hangs a few inches lower and is slightly crooked.

A huge mirror with a majestic wood frame, on the wall directly across from the bed, is incongruent with the rest of the room. The reflection now shows a young child being placed on the bed.

A rusted water pipe at eye level runs along the wall and into the bathroom, serving as a makeshift closet. Several metal hangers, covered with white paper identifying the local drycleaner, hang haphazardly off it. She tosses her damp winter coat in the general vicinity of the hangers and it falls to the floor beneath them.

After putting the baby down on the bed, the woman enters the bathroom with her purchases from the drugstore. She stands in front of the sink and her packages spill out into the basin, knocking a small bar of soap wrapped in thin paper onto the floor. She reaches for the towel hanging on the side of the sink and wipes her brow. After looking in the bags, she takes only the baby oil back to the bed.

She pulls the zipper on the front of the child's sleeper down and draws the infant's hands and feet from the clothing. The kidnapper squeezes a small amount of oil in her hands and begins to rub it around the baby's neck, then between the baby's fingers and toes, but her touch is not gentle and the baby squirms away.

Going back to the shopping bags in the bathroom, the woman withdraws a can of formula and pulls back the tab to open the can. The instructions, WASH HANDS THOROUGHLY, BOIL BOTTLES AND UTENSILS are disregarded. Without diluting the liquid — also part of the instructions — she pours it directly into an unsterilized bottle and attempts to feed the baby. The baby protests the synthetic nipple, and the small amount of gelatinous liquid the baby does swallow immediately upsets her delicate digestive system. Becoming increasingly upset, the baby moves her head back and forth to avoid the bottle being shoved in her face. Subsequent attempts to feed the baby are similarly unsuccessful. The frustrated woman puts the baby back in the knapsack and bundles herself up in her winter coat.

She repeats her trek back to the drugstore.

| CHAPTER 42 |

December 23, 1993
5:00 P.M.

Judi and Kathy, the cashiers for the afternoon shift at the Big V, notice the kidnapper as she enters the store. They watch with heightened awareness as the strange woman proceeds directly to the rack of formula.

Lori, the hospital employee who stopped at the pharmacy on her way home from work, also notices the strange woman as she wanders through the store. Lori quickly makes her way to the checkouts to speak to the cashiers.

"There's that woman again. She is definitely weird, kind of spacey looking," Judi whispers.

"I noticed her right away. She's odd, and seems to be wearing a hospital smock under her coat, like the ones the volunteers are asked to wear. I'm going to walk outside before her, and when she leaves, I'll try to follow her," Lori says, and then rushes into the parking lot.

The kidnapper, still at the formula rack, selects one that reads LACTOSE FREE, INFANT FORMULA FOR COMMON FEEDING PROBLEMS. Unaware that the cashiers are discussing her, she then walks down the hair care aisle, choosing a box of hair dye before proceeding to the checkout.

The cashier tries to get a glimpse of the child, but the woman keeps the baby's face covered. As the employee rings through the purchases, she tries to engage the kidnapper in a conversation. "How are you this evening?"

"I bought the wrong formula when I was here before." The woman digs through the money at the bottom of her purse and begins to count it out.

The pharmacy shares a parking lot with The Bingo Connection, and although there are signs posted in front of the store, advising NO BINGO PARKING IN THIS AREA, they are rarely obeyed. Lori has rushed out to her car, but there is an overflow of vehicles in the pharmacy parking lot and she is blocked in. As she is moving the vehicle back and forth to try to squeeze through an impossibly small space, she sees the strange woman leave the store and take off, walking down the street. Time has run out.

Between customers, Judi and Kathy are trying to look out of the large window behind them, and they see Lori running back into the store.

"I couldn't follow her; someone blocked my car in," says Lori, her eyes wide with concern.

"She said she bought the wrong formula when she was in earlier. Shouldn't a mother know what kind of formula her baby uses?" Kathy replies.

6:00 P.M.

There are no sidewalks, so the kidnapper walks in the bitter cold on the side of the road. A good Samaritan notices the woman with her child and rolls down the car window to ask if she would like a ride. The kidnapper readily accepts but asks the driver to drop her off before she reaches her destination. She thanks her and waves goodbye.

When the driver is out of sight, the woman walks the last few yards and arrives back at room 14 of the Town & Country Motel. She lays the baby on the bed and proceeds to the bathroom with the box of hair dye, balancing gloves and a brush on the small sink as she removes the cap from the bottle of Robust Red to begin her transformation.

About an hour later, the now redhead makes another unsuccessful attempt to feed the baby. The baby doesn't understand her hunger pains. She cries and kicks her little feet. She cries for so long and so hard that she cries herself to sleep. The woman gives up on any effort to feed the child, roughly drops her back on the bed, and walks over to the television, smashing the full bottle of formula down on the dresser.

She turns on the local news station to see if the kidnapping has been mentioned.

| CHAPTER 43 |

December 23, 1993

At 7:00 p.m. a 911 operator receives a call. "911 emergency … fire, police, or ambulance?"

A woman identifying herself as a hospital employee speaks to the operator. "I'm calling about the recent kidnapping at the hospital." The caller tells the emergency operator that she has been shopping at the local pharmacy and has noticed a suspicious woman buying baby supplies. The receptionist takes down the information and forwards it to one of Ford's subordinates for evaluation. The officer decides it is valid information and calls Ford.

Throughout the day, Ford has repeatedly answered the phone, each time hoping that he would receive some information to help him solve this crime. This afternoon, Ford receives some information from his contact within the Child Find organization, which outlined characteristics of a "typical" infant abductor. The data provided is from a study of 256 infant abductions. Although there is no guarantee the infant abductor will fit this description, Ford reads the list:

- The Abductor is usually female of "childbearing" age (range teenager to 53) and often overweight.

- Is most likely compulsive; most often relies on manipulation, lying, and deception.

- Frequently indicates she has lost a baby or is incapable of having one.

- Is often married or cohabitating; companion's desire for a child or the abductor's desire to provide her companion with "his" child may be the motivation for the abduction.

- Usually lives in the community where the abduction takes place.

- Frequently initially visits nursery and maternity units at more than one healthcare facility prior to the abduction; asks detailed questions about procedures and the maternity floor layout; frequently uses a fire-exit stairwell for her escape; and may also try to abduct from the home setting.

- Usually plans the abduction, but does not necessarily target a specific infant; frequently seizes any opportunity present.

- Frequently impersonates a nurse or other allied healthcare personnel.

- Often becomes familiar with healthcare staff members, staff members work routines, and victim parents.

- Demonstrates a capability to provide "good" care to the baby once the abduction occurs.

- Often brings a weapon when planning the abduction, although the weapon may not be used.

As the sergeant puts down the list, he thinks of the many tips he has received.

All of them have been dead ends.

Ford is an imposing figure, towering over six feet tall, with a strong jawline and dark hair that is greying at his temples. He looks uncomfortable in his dark business suit as he sits in his office chair, tapping his desk with a pen. His phone rings yet again, and he listens to the details presented by one of his officers. He hears the story of a woman who purchased baby formula at a pharmacy and then returned to the store a short while later to say that she had purchased the wrong kind. His pen stops tapping as he leans forward in his seat and reaches for a pad of note paper covered with scribbles of information that have been scratched out. He flips to a new page as the officer tells him that this woman had a child with her small enough to be considered a newborn. He learns that the child was being carried around in a knapsack.

"A kid's knapsack?"

"Yeah, like the ones the kids carry books to school in."

Ford makes an indent on the paper as he hastily writes out FORMULA ... KNAPSACK.

He's further told that the woman tried to keep the baby's face covered with a blanket while she was in the store. He writes,

HID BABY and continues to circle his written words. His pulse speeds up. He doesn't waste time hanging up the phone, just uses his finger to push down the button to break the connection and immediately dials out to request the two officers he wants to be sent to the Big V on Plains Road East in Burlington. "Drop what you're doing and get over there, now."

The clock is an incessant, precise reminder of the passing time, and the minutes seem endless before one of the detectives finally calls back.

Ford is aware of the man's excitement before he even speaks, his sharp inhalation hinting at the words to follow. "We may have something here. The woman they are discussing matches the description, and one of the witnesses swears she saw an aqua hospital smock under the suspect's coat."

"Besides the mix-up with the formula, was there anything else strange?"

"This baby she's carrying around in a knapsack, the cashiers think it's small enough to be considered a newborn, yet this woman told them the child was much older."

"Anything else?"

"Yeah. Are you ready for this? She also purchased hair dye."

The lead sounds hopeful, but Ford has learned over the years that hope is often best friends with disappointment. It's not over till it's over and sometimes it's never over. A quick check of the address for the pharmacy puts it in close proximity to the Joseph Brant Hospital. He meticulously takes notes and makes the calls to direct his team of investigators.

He has every available officer in the police department canvassing the streets, looking for Baby Shelby. People have come in on their days off and many others are working double shifts to contribute to the legwork. Among the many searching are Detective Chris Peron and Sergeant Lee-Ann Ansell. Peron stands six feet tall. He has dirty blond hair, a moustache, a youthful face, and a warm smile. Ansell matches him in height and has no-nonsense short red hair. She is one of the officers who have left their homes on their days off to assist in the investigation. Her family has been preparing for a birthday party in her honour, and they now cover up the preparations, putting the celebration on hold.

Ansell has a nine-year-old son and a seven-year-old daughter. They are disappointed that their mom has gone out tonight, and her husband is equally unhappy. Aside from the birthday celebrations, her family was looking forward to spending time together wrapping Christmas presents for under the tree. She tried to explain to the children, "There is a little baby missing. I have to help look for it."

"But mom, it's your birthday!"

"I know, honey, but that baby's mom and dad need my help."

She knows she has to help in the search efforts. She just has to. One more person could make all the difference. What if it were her child? She has to go.

This is the life of a police officer: a never-ending circle of apologies, excuses, and missed family events. Many of her colleague's marriages have not survived the career, and she can sympathize with every one of them. You're damned if you do, and you're damned if you don't.

Peron and Ansell have been working for hours. They were sent to homes in the west end and asked to question some tenants known to the police — some because of past incidents, others because of known histories of mental illness. They have had no success.

The radio gives out a sudden bleat: "All officers in the vicinity of Plains Road East …" They are instructed to check out hotels and apartments in the west end of town, paying close attention to any that are close to the Big V.

| CHAPTER 44 |

An editor at the *Hamilton Spectator* newsroom receives a call from an outside line. He answers, "Newsroom."

The caller's voice is faint and gravelly, like that of a long-time smoker. "I have some information you might be interested in about that kidnapping over at the hospital."

"What can you tell me?"

"The woman … the one the police are looking for …"

"Yes."

"I don't know where she is now …" The statement is followed by a round of coughing. "But I think she might be the person who's renting my basement apartment."

The editor listens closely to the account given by the landlord. He is told that some woman has been renting an apartment in the area of Aldershot, that she has repeatedly fought with her boyfriend and the landlord can often hear them yelling. The landlord heard the tenant tell her boyfriend that she was pregnant. "There's no way that woman is pregnant.…"

The editor has been following the story throughout the day and is well aware of the details, of an infant — a newborn — abducted from her mother's hospital room. He has been visualizing tomorrow's front-page headline: BABY STOLEN. He calls the police and is transferred to Sergeant Ford's line. In his enthusiasm the editor finds it hard to sit still, and he walks a short distance past his desk, stretching the phone cord to its limit.

"Ford here."

The editor identifies himself. He has spoken with the sergeant in the past during other investigations and they are familiar with each other.

"Yes, what have you got for me?"

"About the missing baby … I just received a tip at the news desk, sounds like it might be worth following up on."

"Let's hear it."

"The caller told me that they think they know who the kidnapper is. They said she could be the person renting their basement apartment."

"Why do they think this woman would be the kidnapper?"

"The caller said the tenant has been acting very strange, telling people she's expecting when, as the caller put it, there is no way she could be pregnant. The landlord says not only is she too old to be expecting, you can tell by looking at her that she's not pregnant."

"Was the caller anonymous or did she leave her name?"

"She left her name and her address. It could be someone with an axe to grind or it could be legit. You never know."

"Listen, it would really help if you would sit on this for a while. Give us a chance to check it out."

The newsman could follow up on the lead himself. He should send a camera crew over to the address he has, film the officers arriving. He could release the phone call on the eleven o'clock news. The phone cord goes slack as he walks back around his desk and puts the receiver back in its cradle. When he sits in his black swivel chair, he leans back and puts his hands behind his head and his feet up on the desk. With a stretch and a smile, he "sits on it."

| Chapter 45 |

December 23, 1993
10:30 P.M.

The police cruiser of Detective Chris Peron and Sergeant Lee-Ann Ansell pulls into the Town & Country Motel. An OPEN sign flashes in the window. They slowly drive in a circle around the interior of the property, counting forty rooms. They note there is no room number 13. The room numbers jump from 12 to 14.

There is a dilapidated green link fence at the back of the property with a hand-painted sign that indicates THE POOL IS CLOSED. A bicycle with two flat tires leans against the sign, and plastic summer furniture is randomly scattered around the property.

"Looks like the kind of place that rents rooms by the hour," Peron says as he pulls into one of the many vacant parking spaces. They both exit the vehicle.

When Ansell reaches for the door to the office, she finds it locked. Peering through the glass door, she sees a small black and white television turned on behind the counter. There is a buzzer beside the door, which she rings several times before it is answered. A middle-aged woman, with greying hair, opens the door and looks at them curiously. The officers step in out of the cold and inquire if the motel currently has any occupants matching the description that has been distributed of the kidnapper.

"There's only one lady checked in right now. She wouldn't be the person you're looking for."

"Why's that?"

"She's stayed here before. She doesn't have any baby."

"Can you tell me what room she is in Ma'am?"

"She's in room fourteen"

As the police take their leave, the woman calls after them, "She wouldn't be the one you're looking for," but the police keep on walking and don't respond. She shakes her head, muttering under her breath as she locks the door and goes back to her warm office and the program she is watching.

As they make their way to room 14, Peron's boyish smile is replaced with a look of serious concern. He approaches the door and knocks while Ansell draws near the grimy windowpanes. With one hand on either side of her face, she peers through the gaping curtains. She rests her forehead on the cool pane of glass and sees a woman look over her shoulder toward the door and then move a baby bottle from the top of a dresser to inside one of the drawers. "You're not gonna believe this, but I just saw a woman hide a baby bottle."

Peron knocks a lot harder on the door.

10:45 P.M.

The woman occupying the hotel room is startled by the knock at the door and quickly puts the baby's bottle inside a drawer. She then hurries over and piles all the blankets and a spare pillow on top of the baby. She turns down the television and quietly walks back over to the other side of the room. Standing silently beside the door, she listens, hoping whoever is knocking will go away. She hears another round of knocking, more forceful than the first. She opens the door a crack and finds two people in uniform. "Yes, can I help you?" she asks.

Peron makes the introductions as he holds up his identification. "Miss, I'm Detective Peron and this is my partner Sergeant Ansell. We'd like to ask you a few questions."

Through a small opening in the door, the tenant responds, "What is this about, officer?"

"How long have you been staying at the motel, Miss?"

"Two days ... My husband beat me up yesterday ... I mean, the day before yesterday, and I came here to get away from him."

"Can you tell me your name, Miss?"

"Sarah."

"We can take you to a shelter, Sarah. There are places and people that can help you."

"No, no ... I'm fine now."

Ansell leans into the conversation. "Sarah, we are investigating the recent abduction of a newborn infant from Joseph Brant Hospital. Can we come in and talk to you?"

The woman starts to step back and close the door. "I wouldn't know anything about that. There's no baby here."

"Can we just come in and talk to you for a bit?"

"No. I don't know anything ... I can't help you."

Before the door can be shut in the investigators' faces, Peron tries another tactic. "Okay, thank you, Miss." But instead of turning to leave, he blows into his hands and rubs them together as he asks, "It's really cold out here. Can I come in just for a minute and use your bathroom?"

| CHAPTER 46 |

December 23, 1993
10:45 P.M.

Investigators travel to a home just north of Burlington in Aldershot. The landlord lets them into a basement apartment. The tenant of the rental is long gone, but as they take a walk through the vacant apartment, they find some very peculiar things, including a list of handwritten names — Shirley Megan is written twice and underlined. There is also a birth certificate filled out with the name of Shirley Megan.

Beside the list of names there sits a note.

The investigator looks at the landlord, who has followed them into the apartment. "Did your tenant have a daughter?"

"No, it was just her ... and her boyfriend."

The investigator looks once more at the note in his hand and passes it to his partner, who reads out loud, "Husband, take what you want. I wish you happiness inside your bottle. Merry Christmas. Your Wife and Daughter."

| CHAPTER 47 |

December 23, 1993
11:00 P.M.

At the Town & Country Motel, Detective Chris Peron has persuaded the woman to open the door, and begrudgingly she lets him come in and use the bathroom.

The detectives notice that the television is tuned to the local news.

The woman who has identified herself as Sarah rubs her belly. "I'm pregnant … due in four weeks …"

Peron looks down at her flat stomach as she leads him to the rear of the dingy room and shows him where the bathroom is. "I'm very excited," she says. "Can't wait for the baby to come."

When the door to the bathroom closes, he does a cursory inspection and his suspicions are doubly heightened when he sees a bottle of used hair dye in the garbage can. He comes out of the bathroom and finds the agitated woman waiting for him on the other side of the door. Peron wants to distract the woman. "You're pregnant. When is the big day?" Looking over the woman's shoulder, he gives a nod to his partner, which tells her there is cause to be alarmed.

While the strange woman is preoccupied with her back to Sergeant Lee-Ann Ansell, she takes a quick look around the room and notices a lump in the bed. She hears the woman answer, "January … in a month … The baby is due January twenty-fifth."

Ansell draws back the blankets and finds a motionless baby, its tiny limbs exposed and shiny. Next, her eyes are drawn to what appear to be splashes of blood on the sheets. Ansell fears the worst and reaches over to poke the baby, who stretches and yawns. She has determined that the baby is not in immediate danger.

Peron isn't sure what his partner found, but he knows it's something when he sees Ansell reaching for her handcuffs. As Ansell approaches, the woman turns, and Peron takes hold of the suspect as his partner slaps on the handcuffs. Ansell nods her head, and Chris walks over to the bed. Behind him he hears rights being read:

> You are under arrest for the kidnapping of this infant. You have the right to remain silent. Anything you say can and will be used against you in a court of law. You have the right to have a lawyer present during questioning. If you can't afford a lawyer, one will be provided, at no cost to you. Do you understand these rights?

A detective but also a family man, Peron approaches the bed hesitantly and sees a baby lying very still in crumpled bedding. He also sees the blood on the sheets. He thinks that the baby is dead, so he is ecstatic when the baby opens her red-rimmed eyes and looks at him inquisitively. He then remembers the bottle of red hair dye in the bathroom and puts the pieces together.

After reading the kidnapper her rights, Ansell looks her in the eye. "Why'd ya do it?"

The woman's response is a blank stare. A detective but also a mother, Ansell adds, "If you have hurt that baby ..."

| CHAPTER 48 |

December 23, 1993
11:30 P.M.

Sergeant Lee-Ann Ansell tries to call the police station, but all the lines are busy. She dials 911 and tells the operator she has the abductor and the kidnapped child at the Town & Country Motel.

The local news station receives a live feed of the 911 calls, and within minutes of the call being made to headquarters, notifying of the arrest and rescue, a newscaster is broadcasting the information. Ansell is "blown away" when she hears a voice coming from the television behind her: "And now good news and a happy ending in the story we have been following on the infant abduction from Joseph Brant Hospital."

It takes only minutes for more police to arrive. One officer begins to remove the kidnapper from the motel room. "I did a serious thing, didn't I?" she asks the officer. "I was going to have a Caesarean here."

The detectives share an uneasy glance, realizing she's mad.

"They're going to lock me up for a hundred years, aren't they? They should."

They gently take her arm. "I don't think so," one of them says.

She continues, "It's hard when a man beats you up all the time, especially if he has been drinking and he forgets...." She tries to explain herself, but her words are jumbled and don't make any sense. "My husband has been beating me up and if I didn't bring a baby home I knew he would beat me again."

Nobody says a word, but they are all listening as she keeps talking. "I have just been to the hospital and an ultrasound showed that my baby was dead."

The officers just want to get the woman out of the motel room, but she continues to ramble. "My husband forced me to use a false name in the hospital so they couldn't contact me to make medical arrangements. Last night he beat me so bad I left and took the baby so he would stop beating me."

They have stopped listening. The only thing that matters is that the baby is safe. Ansell goes in one direction, with the baby to the hospital, and Peron goes in the other direction, with the kidnapper.

| CHAPTER 49 |

December 23, 1993
11:30 P.M.

I look at the cellphone beside me on the end table, trying to will it to ring, but it remains silent. When I purchased it, I programmed it with a ring tone of Louis Armstrong singing "It's a Wonderful World." I long to hear it play now and to believe the words are true.

We have one cellphone and this is the number we gave the police. We have two home phones, one in the kitchen and one in the family room downstairs. I pick up the receiver beside me ... Yes, there is a dial tone — it works. Resigned, I place it back in the receiver.

Leaving Glenn and his sister Mary in the family room, I make my way upstairs. The hallways and every corner of the house are dark and full of wanting. I am so tired — tired in body, and tired in spirit, yet my mind won't rest as I make my way through the forest of anxiety that has sprung up in the house. My brain circles like a vulture around one horrible thought after another, but I don't allow it to land on anything. I try to banish any negative reflection and keep my mind blank and my heart full. My love is a beacon, and I send it out with every part of my being to guide Shelby home.

Passing the kitchen, I hear the radio on the counter, tuned to Oldies 1150. "Stay with us tomorrow, when we will be broadcasting up-to-date sightings of Santa Claus as he makes his way through the sky to deliver presents to good girls and boys."

The slow, repetitive drip of the tap echoes in the still room. My throat is dry, but I don't stop to take a drink. The howling of the cold wind outside crescendos, and any thought of thirst disappears.

As I pass by the nursery, I resist the urge to walk inside, yet my eyes drift to the uninhabited crib and I feel an intense emptiness in my being that matches the one within this house. In my heart I feel that Shelby is here, that she's sleeping comfortably. I can almost hear her breathe, but when I look at the crib, I know she's truly gone, and I feel the full impact of loss all over again as I wonder, *What in the world will I do without her?*

Looking in to the children's bedroom, I see that Michael and Caitlin are fast asleep. I think of the book they were read earlier tonight.

> *The children were nestled all snug in their beds,*
> *While visions of sugar plums danced in their heads.*

I pass by their doorway but don't stop to enter. I don't have the energy.

| CHAPTER 50 |

December 23, 1993
11:45 P.M.

The search continues but we have received no information about Shelby, and it is approaching midnight. Everyone has left for the night except for Mary, who has stayed "in case of emergency." No one has dared to voice what that emergency might be. Glenn and Mary now watch the news, each lying on a couch in the family room downstairs.

Glenn is wondering how he will possibly get through the night. Lost in his solitary thoughts, he is startled when the phone rings. When he picks up the receiver, he is surprised to hear the voice of a friend who has contacts at the Hamilton Police

Department. After the friend identifies himself, he says, "Walshie, they've found your baby."

"What the hell are you talking about? How would you know what's going on?"

"I just got a call from a buddy of mine. He told me they found your baby. It's definitely her, Walshie. Don't tell them you heard it from me. They will be calling you shortly, just sit tight."

Glenn has no intention of "sitting tight." As he hangs up the phone, Glenn now hears Jennifer Mossop, from CHCH news, say, "And now good news and a happy ending in the story we have been following on the infant abduction from Joseph Brant Hospital." Mossip's smile is wide and her eyes are bright as she continues, "Police have the kidnapper in custody and the baby has been rescued. We will have more details for you as they are released to the public. Stay tuned."

My sisters and my brother, Chuck, are watching the broadcast from his house. They wonder if they have heard correctly. "Quiet, quiet …," someone says. They gather around and wait for the bulletin to be repeated. My family and the general public hear the news repeated: "We have just heard that there is a happy ending in the case of the kidnapped child from the local hospital. She has been rescued and the kidnapper is in custody."

Glenn immediately gets back on the phone to call his contact, Detective Mike Demeester, in the police department, but reaches an answering machine. Glenn leaves a message: "I have just heard on the news that they have found Shelby. *What is going on?*"

The detective immediately returns Glenn's call. Before Louis Armstrong can start singing, Glenn has the cellphone to his ear. "Yes …"

There is no preamble. "We have her. I wanted to make sure she was all right before I called. She's at Joe Brant now."

Glenn is too overcome to respond. He drops the phone and runs upstairs toward the bedroom.

| CHAPTER 51 |

December 24, 1993
12:00 A.M.

The digital clock on the dresser tells me that it is officially Christmas Eve. I lie motionless beside an empty wooden cradle, which was borrowed from my brother. It housed his four children before being passed on for Michael and Caitlin, keeping them within arm's length during the first tentative weeks of their lives. It's hard to believe that a week ago my biggest worry was that Shelby would be too far away if she slept in the nursery down the hall.

In bed, I am still wearing the clothes I had on at the hospital. I have no will to change them and it just doesn't matter anyway.

Nothing matters except where Shelby is. In desperation I pray. "Please, God ... help me."

"I'll do anything ... just keep her safe."

"Please let me have her back."

"Please, God."

"Please, God."

Have you ever negotiated with God? Have you ever wanted something so bad that you would promise anything to get it? I wish time would just pass. Pass quickly so that the pain will lessen. Pass quickly so that I won't have to live with this uncertainty any longer. Let me wake up when I have the answers.

I can't shut my eyes, and I wonder if I will ever sleep again. I repeat the same prayer over and over, making a multitude of promises — listing the things I will trade for the life of my daughter. I feel like a child myself as I swear, "I will be good, I will be kind, I will never ..." The sound of footsteps running down the corridor interrupts my plea.

My eyes shift toward the door. I am terrified. Glenn enters the room, a dark silhouette, backlit by the hall light. In the dim room, I can't see the expression on his face but I can feel his emotion as strongly as if it were my own. Out of his mouth float the sweetest words I have ever heard, the ones I have been longing to hear. "They've found her."

| CHAPTER 52 |

A moment ago I was too exhausted to stand, and now I feel like I could fly. I am in his arms in an instant, pressed against his chest with my head tucked under his chin. Choked with emotion, he responds to the question I have not yet asked, "She is all right."

We hold on to each other in a crushing embrace. The joy and relief is intoxicating yet sobering at the same time. The life I thought was over has been given back to me. When we separate we quickly make our way down the hall to where Mary is waiting. Glenn confirms that we are going to the hospital and that Mary will watch over the sleeping Michael and Caitlin while we are gone. The phone rings and shatters the conversation.

My heart skips a beat as I reach for the phone on the kitchen counter, and I breathe a sigh of relief when I hear my sister's voice.

She is calling from my brother's house. "We just heard the news. Is it true?"

"Yes, we're on our way to the hospital. Call Mom and let her know what's happening." As my sister conveys the information to the rest of the siblings, I hear a celebration in the background, equivalent to the stroke of midnight on New Year's Eve.

Amidst the screaming and commotion, my sister asks, "Can we come over? We really want to be a part of this."

"Yes, of course … come …" I quickly get off the phone. There is an urgency building. We have to get to the hospital.

Michael and Caitlin are sleeping soundly, oblivious to the roller coaster racing around them, and after as little preparation as we can responsibly get away with, we are ready to leave for the hospital. Mary is going to let our neighbour and the rest of the family know what has happened.

We open the door to exit the house and my brother-in-law Mark is standing there, smiling, on the other side of it. "Your taxi's here!" We laugh and embrace before we follow him to his running vehicle.

Glenn is holding my elbow. We see the puffs of our breath as we step down the icy stairs and make our way to the car. The thought of putting a coat on has not occurred to us. No one asks Mark how he showed up at the exact moment we are walking out the door.

Glenn says, "Joe Brant hospital," as if he is giving instructions to a taxi driver. On the way there, Mark recounts how he was sitting with his elbows on the bar at the local watering hole and social hub The Attic when he heard the news. A cheer went up among the patrons, and Mark shot out of the bar like a bullet — leaving his icy cold glass of beer sitting on the counter, untouched.

I feel lighthearted when I say to him, "Now that's something you don't see every day, you leaving a full beer behind!" I look over at Glenn and say, sweetly, "How was your day, dear?"

Everything is hilarious. We are slap-happy. We are giddy with a combination of amazement and relief. I am frantic to get to the hospital, and Mark cannot drive quickly enough for my liking. "Hurry up," I say. "It's not like anyone is going to give us a ticket!" The frivolity that follows is our way of rejoicing — we laugh and we laugh some more. God, it feels good. Even my inappropriate comment, "It's all fun and games 'till someone loses a child," is met with laughter.

As we get to the top of the Skyway Bridge, the vehicle grows quiet as the mood becomes sombre. The hospital comes into view, and everything appears so tranquil that I wonder if we got the right information, if my child is indeed there. I also start to question whether she is unharmed.

This is the craziest night of my life. I feel manic as the fear and reality begin to creep back in, and my throat tightens. It may be cold outside, but my temperature is rising. I can sense my heart pulsing in my neck, and I can't catch my breath. I feel more than a little nauseated. I take deep breaths and try to swallow the sick feeling — there is no way in hell I am going to ask Mark to pull over so I can throw up.

We enter the hospital parking lot and Mark pulls up to the emergency entrance. We all quickly exit the vehicle. Glenn and I are on a mission. Our desperate need to see our daughter propels us forward. When I enter the hospital it is with a single thought in mind: *Where is she?* Like a heroin addict looking for the next fix, every inch of me is craving relief from the pain of fear and worry. I am frantic to find her.

My eyes scan the emergency waiting room for my daughter. Not an inch goes unexamined. People in chairs that look up at me quizzically, and staff and patients wander by and glance my way. *Where is she?*

Someone is waving me forward. A nurse has recognized us and wants us to follow her. The waters part for me as I follow her gestures down the hall, but my eyes never stop darting back and forth as I systematically case the halls, scouring every face that passes by, overlooking no one and nothing.

I am ushered down a long corridor and into a small room. As the door closes behind me, the sounds of the busy hospital are dulled to a whisper. My whole world has been narrowed to a room that is less than twelve feet wide and fifteen feet long.

An examination table catches my eye, but it is empty. The white countertop is lined with bandages and boxes of medical supplies, and at the end of it is a sink with antibacterial soap. Standing beside the sink are several people with their backs to me. Upon hearing us enter, their conversation stops and they turn around to face us.

Someone has an object in her arms that is wrapped in a blanket, and I am drawn like a magnet. As I grow closer, the fleece covering moves slightly and a gurgle escapes its confines.

I hear a voice in the distance. "I found your baby...."

I approach the arms that are holding the bundle, and someone moves the blanket to reveal the face of a baby. Within a fraction of a second, I take stock of and size up the infant — the tuft of soft blond baby hair, the perfect pink lips, the huge brown eyes that are looking into mine. There are no other eyes like that on the planet.

There is no doubt. It is her. I am home.

| CHAPTER 53 |

Shelby is gently placed in my arms, and I inhale her. I close my eyes and bury my face in her hair as I whisper, "I love you to the sun and the moon and the stars and around the world and back again."

No one exists except for her and me. I feel her surge through my body like an electrical current and the warmth returns to my soul as surely as if I have received an injection of well-being. As the ice in my body begins to melt, I feel my legs starting to give way. A wheelchair is slipped under my knees before I collapse. I immediately open my shirt, tear away the binding, and place her on my breast. She begins nursing with gusto and it is sweet relief. She is looking up at me while she eagerly fills her belly. Our eyes are glued to each other. I think if I could read her mind, she would be asking me where I have been, and I would like to know the same thing of her.

Glenn's hand rests protectively on my back as he and Mark stand behind me, looking over my shoulder. I am oblivious to onlookers. I hear some sniffing and gulping in the room as tears are shed. There is also laughter, the kind that accompanies punch-drunk relief.

After Shelby is satisfied, we go back up to the maternity ward to see if any of the staff is still there from this afternoon, but they are all gone. Like many others they will hear of the rescue from our friends in the media.

It is once again time to leave the hospital. The administrator asks if we brought a car seat for Shelby, but in our rush to get to the hospital, we overlooked putting one in Mark's vehicle. I would like to hold her all the way home, but the administrator finds an infant carrier in the hospital for us to use.

The media have not yet discovered where we are, and the parking lot is quiet. We exit at the emergency entrance, where Mark has pulled up with the van running. Glenn attaches the car seat and securely buckles Shelby inside. I get into the van and relish the sound of the heavy metal door as it slides in place, locking us safely inside.

Glenn and Mark are in the front, and I am sitting beside Shelby in the back — so close you could not put a piece of paper between us. I would like to crawl right into the baby seat with her, but holding her hand will have to suffice until I get her home. I catch Glenn's eye in the rear-view mirror. Our gaze lingers before we both look toward the baby seat. Shelby has had a busy day. She sleeps.

| CHAPTER 54 |

December 24, 1993
3:00 A.M.

We are home with Shelby. My brother and sisters greet us at the door with open arms. They started celebrating the minute they got to our house. The good cheer is brightly circling around the room like fireflies, lighting the corners and hallways that were so dark earlier this evening. The house is now infused with the wonderful familiar sounds of conversation and laughter.

We barely fit as we all head down the hall together to wake up Michael and Caitlin. The children had the option of having their own rooms but have always chosen to bunk together. Michael is on the top of a set of bunk beds with his blankets kicked off and his arm lazily hanging over the protective shield that prevents him from falling. Caitlin is on the bottom bunk, snug as a bug in a rug, in her pink nightie.

An octopus of arms reaches for them. "Wake up, Michael. Wake up, Caitlin. They found Shelby!"

Two sleepy heads open their eyes and grin dopey smiles. Michael says, "They did…? Is she okay?"

"Have a look for yourself, she's fine," Glenn says.

Caitlin is rubbing her eyes while Glenn lifts her out of bed, and her little legs wrap around his waist.

Michael and Caitlin are quick to bend over their sister with baby talk, hugs, and sloppy kisses. After a brief visit, we shepherd them back off to bed. Caitlin says, "Did they find the bad lady?"

"Yes, they found the bad lady."

"Is she in trouble?"

"Yes, she's in *big* trouble."

Michael and Caitlin smile at each other. Someone is in trouble and they are not.

The children say their goodnights and the familiarity of their words warms my heart. "Night Momma, night Dad."

After Caitlin says goodnight to Michael, she predictably yawns and curls up with her little bottom in the air to go immediately back to sleep. She murmurs, with her eyes closed, "Night Shelby." The resiliency of children is a marvel.

My family is ready to party, but I want to sleep for a year.

I'd like to bring Shelby to bed with me, but my family steps in and says it's not a good idea. Glenn takes her in his arms and walks me down the hall to our bedroom. I don't have the energy to remove my clothes, so I just crawl into bed with them still on, and Glenn pulls a blanket over me before he leaves the room. I've ridden a wave that has taken me from extreme low to extreme high, and although I'm back in calm water, I can still feel the motion sickness.

I lie in bed, listening to the cheerful voices of my family

drifting down the hall, but my fatigue prevents me from processing what is being said. I just hear sound, and that slowly fades as I drift off to sleep.

| CHAPTER 55 |

December 24, 1993
6:30 A.M.

We are awoken by a persistent knock at the door. My sister, who is sleeping on the couch, answers and is met with a microphone and a barrage of questions. "Can we ask you some questions about the kidnapping?" "Will the mother or father have a few words with us?" "How is the baby? Can we get a photo of her?" "Do you know why the kidnapper did it? Did you know her?"

Behind the owner of the microphone is a person with a camera pointed at my sisters' face. She looks beyond them and sees several white news vans with satellite dishes protruding from them. She doesn't know what to do, so she quickly closes the door.

Standing a few feet behind her, we look on in amazement.

The press go back to their respective vans and, like hunters, they wait for any movement within the house. Their cameras are pointed like guns at the thick lace curtains drawn shut in the living room. They can see silhouettes moving behind them, and they are taping the shadows as a reporter speaks into a microphone and gestures toward our home.

It has begun.

We live in a quiet neighbourhood. A big maple tree with three pieces of two-by-four hammered into the trunk grows in our front yard — the makeshift ladder permits easier climbing. The tree is now covered with Christmas lights, and the bulbs hang slightly askew as the lower limbs, encased in ice, bend and dip from the extra weight. A basketball net at the end of the driveway shows the wear of hundreds of missed shots. Depending on the season, haphazardly placed bicycles, wagons, or sleds usually decorate our front yard. We ordinarily see no traffic on our street except for the handful of people who live in our cul-de-sac. Today, however, our identity has been made public and there is a hubbub of activity.

Our home is a modest red brick bungalow, not grand, but blessed with everything that matters inside. Today, when a family member enters or leaves the house they are approached and questioned by reporters. The media is respectful but unrelenting. They have a job to do and a story to cover. The phone has been ringing non-stop with calls from various papers and news stations.

The interest in our story is intense and widespread. Everyone can relate to a child going missing: all parents at one time or another have lost sight of their child. It may have been for seconds or perhaps minutes, but they nonetheless understand the emotion of fear associated with a missing child.

A neighbour of mine once recounted a story to me of when her children were playing hide-and-seek outdoors. When she called them in for dinner, one of her sons did not answer. He was five years old at the time, and she looked for him but could not find him. Her other children did not know where he was. No one could find him. She was frantic and called the police. After a search of the neighbourhood, her son was discovered behind the bushes in her yard. He had lain down during his turn to hide, and while his brother was looking for him, he had fallen fast asleep. That day still haunts her.

Many people have a vested interest in the story, and they want to hear what the reporters have to say.

Members of the press continue to approach the house and ask if they can come in and speak to us. There are many different pleas, some more creative than others.

It's hard to know what to do. There are so many people with so many questions that it is all very overwhelming, and it's almost impossible to leave the house.

The doorbell rings and this time it is the Vlaikov family, who own The Attic. They heard about the press on our street and have made their way through the crowd to bring pizzas for the family.

We communicate constantly with the police sergeant, who believes that the best solution is to hold a press conference to answer people's questions. He suggests that we don't delay it, and he plans it for today at 1:00 p.m. We agree to go to the local police headquarters, and the media is notified. The press depart from our front lawn and the vans drive away down the street.

| CHAPTER 56 |

December 24, 1993
1:00 P.M.

Glenn's brother Wayne becomes our chauffer and official bodyguard. With Shelby in my arms, Glenn and I enter the publicity room. We are taken aback by the commotion and sheer volume of media. Flashing lights blind us. We don't register individual faces, just a sea of people with a common goal: get the details of the story.

With limited sleep since the kidnapping and rescue, my legs, already shaky, turn to rubber. Glenn takes my arm and helps me into a seat beside him. We sit at a long table, similar to the head table at a wedding except the press is sitting where our guests would be, and where there should be place settings there are microphones and tape recorders. The police who were involved in the search and rescue support us on either side. It is hot beneath the bright lights that have been set up for video footage and photography.

Sergeant Joe Martin of the force's Media Relation Unit has interrupted his vacation to come in and handle the heavy media coverage over the next few weeks. He opens the conference with a welcome and the facts. It is eerily quiet as the film rolls and the cameras are poised for snapshots.

"Yesterday at or about noon, a woman entered the hospital dressed as a nurse ..."

I start to drift away in my own thoughts, but I catch the odd sentence as he recounts a brief summary.

"Two of our detectives went to the Town & Country Motel ..."

Every so often someone will move beside or behind us and snap a picture of Shelby. The rolling film catches her flinching when the flash goes off.

"... the child was unharmed and taken to the hospital to be examined before being released to her parents earlier this morning.

"The woman was arrested. We have been interviewing her throughout the early morning. We have had some difficulties, as she was not identifying herself. We have several names for this woman, but we feel we now have the accurate name for her. She is forty-eight years of age, and she does match the description of the suspect seen at the hospital directly after the kidnapping. She has been charged with kidnapping, and she will be appearing for a bail hearing at 1:30 this afternoon. I will tell you that she has only been in this area for two weeks. Prior to that she was in the provinces of New Brunswick and Newfoundland, and that is about as far back as we have been able to trace her at this point. She was originally from the U.S.A. With respect to the parents and ourselves, we are very, very pleased with the outcome of this incident."

The floor is opened for questions. They start firing in rapid succession, and we do our best to answer. "How did you feel when you realized your baby had been kidnapped? What did you do when you got home? What did your other children do when you told them what happened?"

Glenn answers, "They took it better than I expected they would. I was tortured with how I was going to tell them what happened...."

I look up at him and I don't think I have ever loved him more. It seems to me that we are each other's glue right now. I am asked a question and get halfway through the answer and stop. When I feel myself choking up, I look up at him, and with an unspoken understanding he finishes my sentence. It's a beautiful thing when you know each other so well that you can finish one another's thoughts.

When it comes to the questions of what actually happened to me in the hospital, I freeze. "What did the kidnapper say and what did she do?"

There is silence as everyone waits for my response. You could hear a pin drop. I can't answer. I understand that people are curious, but I can't answer. The pain is still too raw and I'm so tired and sleep deprived that I am afraid I don't have the strength to keep my composure. I don't want to cry in front of all of these strangers, and so I swallow and take big gulps of air to steady myself. My fingers are gripping Shelby's blankets. I keep looking down at her, waiting for the moisture to clear from my eyes. I caress the soft tendrils of hair from her forehead. As I look up at Glenn, I see he is also hanging on by a thread. "She was very smooth. I can't be more specific right now," I say.

Glenn closes with a statement. "I want to publicly thank everyone that has supported us through this ordeal. Our family ... the police that have worked so hard, all of the people who called in tips, the cashiers at the drugstore ... we are grateful to everyone for their assistance."

The CBC closes the broadcast with, "Our top story today, Baby Shelby, a portrait of sweet innocence, sleeps while two very exhausted parents revisit the nightmare."

As the other journalists close their broadcasts, we adjourn to a back room with the group of police officers who participated in the efforts to bring Shelby home. They give us a huge white teddy bear wearing a scarf embroidered with the police department initials, and we keep it in her crib to watch over her while she sleeps for the next two years. Photographs are again taken and we see them the following day in the paper with the heading POLICE UNIT HONOURED FOR WORK, BABY SHELBY FOUND SAFE AND SOUND THANKS TO TEAM SPIRIT.

1:30 P.M.

The kidnapper is taken to the justice of the peace and presented with the charge of kidnapping. When the name of the child is read out, she interjects, "She's Megan."

The accused confirms that she understands the charges.

| CHAPTER 57 |

We live in a small town. It seems like everyone knows one another — there are no six degrees of separation. Entering one of the local pubs in the neighbourhood guarantees our small gathering becomes a large one. Our children play with the children of people we went to school with. We know the families that own the local businesses and the people that work for them by name. There has always been a comfort to this familiarity, but now I long for anonymity.

Now that the media is no longer camped outside my front door, I decide to get some fresh air and go to the store to get milk and bread. The last thing I want to do is speak to anyone. My plan for the future entails drifting through the next few days, weeks, years unnoticed. I want time to heal and space to do it in.

I'm feeling edgy, like everyone is looking at me. I wonder if this is what agoraphobia feels like. If I walk into the store with my head down, no one will notice me and I can just grab what I need and make a hasty exit. As I walk through the door of the local convenience store, the Elm King Variety, I notice Shelby's face plastered across the front pages of every newspaper on the stand. They have used the pictures that we gave to the police in the initial frenzy of her kidnapping. These pictures were taken on my camera: they are mine, they belong to me and my family, they are not meant to be used like this.

Below the words MERRY CHRISTMAS the headlines read:

Hamilton Spectator: BABY RESCUED, HAPPY CHRISTMAS HAS NEW MEANING FOR FAMILY OF KIDNAPPED GIRL.

Toronto Star: POLICE HUNT 5-DAY-OLD BABY SNATCHED FROM HOSPITAL BED.

Toronto Sun: BABY FOUND, WOMAN SNATCHED 5-DAY-OLD GIRL FROM HOSPITAL IN BURLINGTON; COPS DISCOVER SHELBY ALIVE AND WELL.

During the time I was dependent on my parents, I moved nine times and went to four different schools. I had a lot of friends in a lot of different neighbourhoods, but no matter how close I felt to a friend, I never told them what went on behind all those closed doors.

As children we rely on our parents to set an example. The example I followed was secrecy. When faced with adversity in the past, it was my decision what I chose to share and very likely the choice was silence. Exercising this option gave me some control over my life. Now I have none.

These papers have a distribution count of well over a million copies nationwide. The privacy that I have coveted all of my life is a thing of the past, and the community is privy to the most private moments of the worst day of my life.

Only a handful of people mingle in the store, but I feel their eyes on me. Hobbling over to the cooler, I pick up a bag of milk. Passing the bread display, I scrunch a loaf under my arm. Self-consciously, I reach for a copy of each of the newspapers and place some bills on the counter. Keeping my gaze straight ahead, I hurry out of the store.

| CHAPTER 58 |

At the end of a day that has seemed like a week, Glenn leaves to go to the traditional midnight Mass at St. Francis Xavier Parish in Stoney Creek, the same church he has been visiting since he was two years old. His parents used to bring all seven of their children to church every Sunday, and together they would wiggle and squirm through the hour-long service. He dips his hand in the holy water at the entrance to the church and makes the sign of the cross. He is surrounded by the stained glass windows that line the sides of the church, spilling colours of red and blue and yellow across the sanctuary. The pews shine from the thousands of times they have been polished, not only by working hands but also by the bottoms of the faithful. Tattered hymnals and Books of Worship are within easy reach. The fans rotate on the cathedral ceiling, but they do little to move the air around the large space. At the front of the church, a detailed, life-sized crucifix hangs behind the altar.

On Christmas Eve the church is always full to capacity. People stand along the sides and back of the church. Most are dressed in their Sunday best, yet a few break tradition and loosen their coats to reveal jeans and a lack of adornment. Despite the crowd and the heat of the fully packed room, Glenn feels the peace of his surroundings and a calm that he has not felt since his last visit. Parents behind him are shushing their children to be quiet as the priest makes his way down the centre aisle.

The organ music and the angelic voices of the children's choir drift downward. "God gave us the power to love and understand, to reach out with our hearts to our fellow man." A few of the curious children peak down at the crowd through the gleaming wooden banister on the balcony above.

As Glenn settles into a pew, the priest begins his sermon to the congregation. "My dear friends, yesterday in our small town a child was taken from its family … kidnapped by a stranger." There is silence as the priest continues, "We saw a community come together in prayer and with purpose. We witnessed mankind at its worst."

Glenn looks up to the statue of Jesus on the cross. He stares at the blood below Jesus's rib where he was pierced with a spear and the blood on his forehead from the crown of thorns. He sees pain and sadness.

The priest has more to say on the matter. "We witnessed mankind at its best." His eyes connect with Glenn's, and for a fleeting moment it's like he is speaking to him alone. "We are reminded of the hope, faith, and love that Jesus has given to millions and millions of people throughout history."

The priest has no idea that the family he speaks of belongs to his parish or that the father of the kidnapped child is listening to his words. He continues to praise the goodness of people and the hard work and determination that went into finding this child.

"Thanks be to God, the child was rescued and is now safe in the bosom of its family."

He asks for the congregation to join in a prayer of healing for the family. His voice is strong and reverential as he speaks of forgiveness and the Christmas spirit of hope and love that is present today as it was this day in Bethlehem.

The congregation turns to number 563 in their Book of Worship and sings, "Sing a New Song unto the Lord; let our song be sung from mountains high." As the parishioners continue to raise their voices in song, the candles flicker and the beauty of the church adds to the overall feeling of warmth. The children join in the singing: "Rise, O children from your sleep; your saviour now has come. He has turned your sorrow into joy and filled your soul with song."

Standing beside the altar, which is draped in starched white linen, the priest continues his sermon, looking at the Bible held by a beautiful dark-haired boy with fair skin. With steady hands, the child heeds every movement of the priest, who now raises his eyes and says, "May the peace of the Lord be with you always. At this time we will offer a sign of peace to one another." Everyone in the crowded room turns to their neighbour and grasps their hand, repeating the words "Peace be with you," and their fellow Christian replies, "Peace be with you."

At the end of the service, Glenn waits for the crowd to disperse and approaches the priest. "Father ... it was my child ... the child you spoke of that was kidnapped. It was my child."

The priest is momentarily speechless. "God bless you, my son."

When Glenn returns home from church, all the lights in the house are out except for the ones on the Christmas tree. I am in the rocking chair, nursing Shelby. I look up as he enters. His eyes are bright when he says to me, "Guess what the sermon was about tonight...?"

| CHAPTER 59 |

December 25, 1993
Christmas Day

I was up most of the previous night doing one of two things: feeding Shelby or waking from nightmares that leave me breathless. This will become a persistent pattern in my life as my dreams continue to pollute my waking moments.

When we dream, we enter a world that is all our own. In my dreams nothing is as it should be and everything has a secret meaning that is slightly beyond my grasp. The monkeys from *The Wizard of Oz*, which terrified me as a child, are frequently part of my dreams, and they chase my family around. Whenever the monkeys catch someone, that person becomes a creepy monkey and joins in the ranks of the ones chasing. First they catch my grandmother, who already resembles a little hunched over monkey, and I watch her transform completely. She leads the pack, chasing after my mother, my brother, and my sisters until I have no one left.

I am now the only one who is not a monkey. I want to run to avoid being caught by the monkeys, but my feet are heavy as lead and they won't move quickly. I find a bicycle with a banana seat. It has a bell on the handlebars, and I ring it as I go through traffic. I make my way to the hospital, with coloured streamers flowing from the handlebars and baseball cards folded in the spokes of the wheels, making engine noises. I know that at the hospital I will be reunited with Shelby, and when I enter I see a doctor. I believe she has Shelby in her arms. I reach for my child, and just when things are starting to make sense, the doctor hands me a package that is wrapped in brown butcher paper. It is damp and dripping something red. The package is small and round — about the size of a grapefruit ... or a head. As I am tearing at the paper to open it, the package slips from my hands and falls between the floorboards that have started to give way. Through the gaps in the floor, I see a number of skulls, partly deteriorated but with mouths moving, trying to tell me something that I can't understand.

I want to go home. There are so many past houses. I don't remember where I live. I am transported to a long distorted corridor that leads to my children's bedroom. When I finally reach their bedroom, at the end of the hallway, I discover empty bunk beds with blankets in shreds. The bedroom window is open and snow covers the floor. The curtains are swaying in the wind, and I hear multiple voices repeating, "She's in shock, she's in shock." A familiar person whispers in my ear, "I'll take good care of them."

I wake up in a cold sweat. At this point I have decided the children will not sleep with their windows open — ever — and I may even go so far as to nail them permanently shut. I have begun to crave the dreamless sleep that once left me rested and refreshed.

Today, my sister Maureen hosts Christmas dinner for the whole family.

The turkey comes out of the oven, golden brown and overflowing with homemade stuffing — the kind of stuffing that's crammed with sausage, mushrooms, apples, carrots, onions, celery, and lots of savory. The potatoes, whipped with gobs of butter and cream, wait for the thick brown gravy. The turnips, mashed with brown sugar, sit beside the corn and Brussels sprouts in CorningWare bowls. The homemade pies of mincemeat, apple, and blueberry line the counter. The smells waft through the house. The dishes and pots clang in the kitchen.

Surrounded by brightly wrapped presents, we listen to Bing Crosby singing Christmas carols: "I'll be home for Christmas, just you wait and see."

I sit in the corner with Shelby in my arms, a place where she will spend most of her infancy. If she is not in my arms, she is being held by someone else. I sometimes wonder how she will ever learn to walk. Even though I am surrounded by the people I love and the abundance of the season, I am fighting tears and swallowing the sobs I feel building in my chest.

I have fears that I never had before. I'm suspicious of people that I used to trust. I have lost the rose-coloured glasses that I was so often accused of wearing. This saddens me. I feel a tear escape, and its warmth runs down my cheek, the wet path cooling my skin before it drops onto my white blouse.

I look down at Shelby and marvel that someone tried to steal my baby. The wrongdoer put thought and effort into the execution of the plan and almost got away with it. I can't understand who would do such a thing and why. I don't think animals ever take the newborns of another animal — I've only heard stories of humans committing such an atrocity. This person consciously made the decision to steal another woman's child. She made the choice to break someone's heart and mind. Now that my family is safe I have a million questions that remain unanswered.

Quieter than our usual get-togethers, there are reserved conversations going on around the room.

When we are all seated at the table, Maureen makes a toast in a voice trembling with emotion. "To family."

Everyone raises their glasses and repeats, "To family."

I am beginning to realize that this ordeal is not over for my family. The pebble has been dropped and the ripples will continue.

| CHAPTER 60 |

On February 14, 1994, the trial begins for us, along with our education in the judicial system. We visit previously uncharted territory of legal jargon, criminal prosecution, and defence proceedings.

The lawyer for the prosecution is Richard Garwood-Jones, assistant Crown attorney. His distinguished name suits him. He is tall, dark, and handsome, impeccably dressed in a manner befitting a lawyer. He is not the kind of man you would ever picture being referred to as Rick.

After the accused was apprehended and taken to jail, her case appeared in the open docket for assignment by the Crown attorney's office. Fortunately for us, Richard Garwood-Jones had been interested in the incident from the onset and requested to represent the Crown attorney's office as the lead counsel.

In the gallery, we sit with the detectives who have been working on the case. The investigators are like bookends holding Glenn and me up against the stares and curiosity of the crowd. The uncomfortable benches remind me of church, as do the smells of polished wood and wet winter coats. The crowd holds very few familiar faces. Many of the people in attendance have paper and pen in hand and are looking on expectantly. The silence builds as everyone waits for the proceedings to start.

Glenn looks over at me and whispers, "Is that her?"

The accused is led into the courtroom dressed in a bright green skirt and top. I can't speak or take my eyes off her. I nod. This is the first time that I have seen the Shadow since she walked out of the hospital room with my baby in her arms. I hate her. I hate her with all my might. I am willing her to look back at me, but she does not glance my way. My heart is thumping out of my chest. Someone who has threatened and hurt my family is within arm's reach. Animal instincts kick in and the rage comes to the surface. Looking over my shoulder, I see my sister sitting behind me in the courtroom. Our eyes meet and I feel her support from across the crowded room. I think she understands how I feel.

I remember experiencing this kind of rage toward *one* other person who hurt and threatened my family when I was fourteen years old. Perhaps my sister is thinking the same thing. My mind wanders to the past — a place that is all right to visit but not where I want to live.

I remember when my sister was a child of eleven. I entered our bedroom to find it eerily quiet, with the curtains drawn. Although it was sunny outside, darkness permeated the room. My sister was watching the doorway. She was doing nothing else. Tormented by her thoughts, she sat still, watching the entrance to the bedroom. When I walked in and looked into her eyes, I could see that something had changed.

Her face was a canvas of emotions, revealing a combination of fear and revulsion. She sat amongst a pile of crumpled bedding that she had gathered around her like a shield. She had been waiting for me; the story spilled out of her. My little sister had been sexually abused by a neighbour. She recounted the details of what was done to her. I was shocked and sickened. It broke my heart to see the pain she was in and to realize she had lost her innocence. I felt her words as much as I heard them.

At the time she was abused, I felt a loathing toward the person who assaulted her and I experienced anger in a way that I never had before and thought I never would again. My fury knew no bounds. Although I was just a child myself, I contemplated revenge in many forms, and if I thought I could have gotten away with it, I would have carried out my own retribution. Nothing is more painful than witnessing the suffering of a loved one and my heart overflowed with not only a deep love for her but also a bitter agony — an agony not unlike the one she felt for me when my baby was kidnapped.

In the end I convinced my sister that we had to tell our parents. He had to be punished; he had to be stopped from hurting anyone else. She reluctantly agreed, and I went and told my mother what had happened. That's when all hell broke loose. Mom told Dad. I don't think he wanted to believe it. He came flying into the room where she and I were sitting on the bed and said, "You better be telling the truth …"

He stood and looked at my sister while he waited for a response that never came. I didn't like my father very much at that moment. He stormed out of the room while finishing his sentence, "… because we're calling the police." The sound of cursing could be heard slowly receding down the hall with him.

The police were called, the details were rehashed, and salt was poured on the wound every time my sister was questioned. The questions were hard for her to answer, as she didn't even know the proper words to use when describing how her body was violated.

Sometime later the man was formally charged. He went to trial, all spiffed-up in his Sunday's best with a lawyer. Her attacker pled guilty and was convicted in a court of law. As was typical at the time, the court looked favourably on his admission of guilt, and he received a year's probation. Only twelve months of inconvenience for the atrocities he had committed against my sister.

It is still with considerable difficulty that I swallow this fact. Given what is known about the probability of sex offenders repeating their abhorrent behaviour, I can only wonder about the heinous crimes that he may have committed both before and after he robbed my sister of her childhood. The story never left the courtroom, and he was free to walk the streets with no one the wiser, perhaps even befriended by his neighbours. As is common after a sexual assault, no one ever acknowledged publicly what happened to my sister. The outrage remained invisible. To the world, she was not a victim and her assaulter was guilty of nothing. A double injustice occurred, the first when she was wronged and the second when the crime disappeared as if it never happened. The problem is that you can't heal a wound that you deny even exists. My youngest sister would carry this burden for the rest of her life.

Back in the courtroom, where the kidnapper is being tried, I wonder if the judicial system will work for us in this case. Will the judge award an appropriate sentence? Emotions run high when a crime has been committed. It's understandable why some people have made the mistake of taking the law into their own hands — sometimes it seems to make a whole lot of sense.

I lean toward one of the sergeants, but my eyes do not leave the accused. "Would it be possible for me to speak with her ... alone?"

I visualize the scene in my mind: *I wait until the detective leaves the room. I look over my shoulder to make sure he's gone. I leap over the desk I imagine would be separating us. I curl my fingers to form a fist, keeping my thumb on the outside the way Glenn has shown me. I pull my arm back to build momentum ...*

The sergeant responds to my inquiry with a smirk. "Diana, you know there are no metal detectors in this courtroom."

Is he insinuating I could have brought a gun?

"Can I speak to her?" I ask again. The sergeant's smirk slowly subsides as he realizes I'm serious.

"We would have to accompany you."

Well, that sort of defeats the purpose.

The subject is dropped as the bailiff starts the day. "All rise, as the Right Honourable Justice Patrick Lesage enters the courtroom."

| CHAPTER 61 |

During the opening statements, the defence attorney notes that the accused will be pleading guilty to the charge of kidnapping. He explains that the early plea is to spare the victims further grief.

He tries, to no avail, to give some justification for the actions leading up to the kidnapping: "She decided to kidnap Baby Shelby after a fight with her common-law husband, when both had been drinking. Hoping to end this abuse, she had told her common-law husband she was pregnant ... Her landlady heard her say, 'Don't hit me, I'm eight months pregnant.'

"The accused was deeply in love with her common-law husband." The details grow increasingly bizarre. "Knowing that her common-law husband had fathered a child with his brother's wife, she thought he might treat her better if she were pregnant.

Once she concocted the fictitious pregnancy, she felt like she was backed into a corner. She had a couple of drinks and set out for the hospital. She never intended to harm this young child.

"The accused is greatly impacted by this trial. She is suffering at the thought of what pain her actions are causing her own family."

The accused dabs her eyes with a tissue.

Continuing, the lawyer says, "The kidnapper's daughter has lost respect for her and her adoptive parents are also very hurt."

The trial has now shifted. The judge is not here to determine guilt or innocence, but to decide the fate of the offender. What is an appropriate punishment for a woman who has pled guilty to kidnapping a newborn infant, from the child's mother, in the maternity ward of a hospital — a place that the community has always considered safe?

Defence lawyer Richard LeDressay asks the court to impose a sentence of two years less a day. LeDressay is by all accounts an honourable man. We all have a right to a defence, and he is just doing his job, yet it is still impossible not to dislike him. He became the enemy when he painted a picture of the kidnapper as a victim and tried to justify her actions. There is a quiet buzz in the courtroom as the lawyer takes his seat.

Prosecutor Richard Garwood-Jones rises and gives his opening statement. He recounts all of the steps that were taken leading up to the crime. His aim is to show the amount of cunning and forethought that went into the crime, to describe how it was neither a crime of passion nor impulse. The kidnapping of this child involved weeks and even months of calculated planning.

He slowly and meticulously outlines the timeline of the accused. He begins with before the kidnapping on December 16, when she opened a new bank account with a fictitious name, address, and occupation, and he proceeds to the preparations made in the days leading up to the kidnapping on December 23. He recounts her actions moments before she entered the hospital room, how she slipped her hands into a pair of latex gloves before entering the maternity ward. He tells the court what she did with her time after leaving the hospital, right up to the time she was apprehended by the police.

Convictions for breaking and entering, fraud, assault, and possession of a weapon are cited from a previous criminal record. His statement describes a woman with a history of making bad decisions that include deceit and violence. I want to stand up and clap — *that's more like it!* Prosecutor Richard Garwood-Jones asks the court to impose a seven-year prison term.

Several witnesses are called to the stand, including one of my sisters, who gives a victim impact statement. She tells how this unlawful act has continued to affect her and others in a negative way. She gives examples of her hypervigilance with her own children, how she panics after they get on the bus to leave for school, and how she checks their beds at night after they have gone to sleep. She then steps down, and I am called to the stand to also give a victim impact statement.

Looking straight ahead, I make the walk from my seat to the front of the courtroom and slide into the small enclosed wooden bench that serves as the witness box. I feel like I'm the one on trial.

I am asked to describe how this event has affected my life and my family. In the hushed courtroom, I attempt the impossible explanation. "I can't believe I almost lost my child. I literally handed her over from my breast and loving arms to the arms of a stranger."

I explain that I have lost my trust in people and can't see myself ever getting it back. I tell them how I have changed in ways that I don't like and I am not the same person I was a year ago.

I tell them how I wake up screaming from nightmares, and that my health has been affected by the sleep deprivation. The memory impairment caused by the trauma is a constant source of frustration and embarrassment to me. My voice is the only sound in the courtroom as I detail the impact this crime has had throughout the country and the correspondence I have received from perfect strangers expressing their anxiety, grief, and outrage.

A hospital, once thought to be one of the safest environments in the community, is now feared by many expecting mothers. I recognize that my child was rescued because of the hard work of the police, the media, and the community, and not through any change of heart on the part of the kidnapper.

My child is back not because she was *returned* to me but because she was *rescued*. My life would have been a disaster if she had not been. I would have been like so many other parents who have not had the good fortune to be reunited with their children. When I am finished speaking, there is silence in the courtroom.

Justice Lesage leans over and looks directly into my eyes. He speaks quietly, compassionately, in a consoling way. "There is nothing that you would have been expected to do. You were purely the victim of a crime."

The judge's comment disarms me. I want to respond with something eloquent — a simple thank you, but I am choked up and can't find the words. I want to get out of this constricting witness box and out of this courtroom. I want to lie on the couch in my living room, under a cozy afghan with a cup of tea and a good book to escape from the crime novel I am now in the middle of, but I say nothing, merely nod my head in response.

The judge calls a recess, and this gives us all time to compose ourselves after a very arduous morning. As I walk back to my seat, I pass an artist who has sketched a drawing of me on the witness stand. There are no cameras allowed in the courtroom, and this sketch is later seen on the six o'clock news along with all the sordid details that are now in the public domain.

When we leave the courtroom, we see members of the press running to the telephones in the hall. Reporters have a deadline to submit stories for tomorrow's paper, and they will share whatever details they can with the typists waiting patiently to start their columns. I catch snippets of conversations as I walk down the hall.

"... fight with her common-law husband. They had been drinking ..."

"... previous criminal record ..."

I see a pretty blonde woman whom I recognize from television broadcasts. She looks up as I pass mid-sentence: " ... taken from her breast and loving arms." She has the good grace to blush and look away as she realizes I have overheard her conversation.

When the day draws to a close, we drive home to the children, who are being cared for by a long-time friend. It is the first time that the children have been left with anyone but us since the kidnapping. We turn on the car radio, and while we drive we listen to the updates from today's court proceedings.

| CHAPTER 62 |

The next day, court resumes. The prosecutor presents a videotape that was confiscated from the hospital. The recording shows the kidnapper leaving with a baby in her arms. It is shown about a dozen times. Over and over and over, I watch the kidnapper leaving the hospital with my daughter in her arms. I want to scream, "All right already!"

There is so much that I want to remember but can't. Now here is something I would like to forget and I am being forced to relive it. I want to grab the remote and crush it under my foot. I am powerless, and as the dust particles drift in front of the television screen, I watch the video like everyone else in the room.

There is no mistaking her identity. The prosecutor has made that perfectly clear to everyone in the courtroom. Further evidence is shown that validates all of the prosecutor's previous statements:

documentation to register the birth of a new baby, hospital clothing and supplies for collecting blood, as well as the sign that was posted on the library door indicating a meeting in progress, all found in the dumpster behind the local Zellers.

The accused has prepared a statement and now has the opportunity to present it.

"Your Honour," the defence attorney says, "my client would like to say a few words."

The accused stands and faces the judge. Not once during the trial will she look at me. Not once will we speak to each other. She calmly starts to read from a piece of yellow foolscap in her hands: "I have entered a guilty plea because I am guilty, but I also wanted to spare all of the victims any further trauma. I am very remorseful for my crime. Baby Shelby is safe and with her parents as God wanted. I have a daughter too, but through all of this I lost her love and respect — my pain, my loss, I bear forever."

She stops reading and looks down at the ground. When she looks once again at her paper she says, "My son …" and pauses.

We all wait for her to continue, but she hands the paper over to her lawyer and sits down. The defence attorney continues reading as the kidnapper sits hunched over in her seat: "My son, Jeff, said, 'What happened to the mom I knew?' My parents are the two most beautiful people anyone would be so lucky to know, married sixty-four years, well-respected and beloved in their community. Again, the anguish brought upon them by all this is my pain and my loss. A judgement of death here or one hundred years in prison could not be as painful as what my heart and conscience must bear for the rest of my life."

Court is adjourned for a recess while the judge deliberates on sentencing. His response at the end of the trial is as follows:

> The accused read a statement that was finished
> by her counsel as she was in an emotional state.
> She has committed a most heinous crime. She

is not an evil person, but she has committed an evil crime. The crime of kidnapping, especially the kidnapping of a young child, is one that we, as citizens, have no reasonable way of protecting ourselves from. Kidnapping by a stranger in Canada is, thank God, not a common crime but it is so shockingly evil that when it occurs a denunciatory or an exemplary sentence must be imposed. Society simply cannot react to this crime except with a sentence that will deter other persons who might consider doing the same. What she did was stupid and senseless but she does not suffer from a mental illness. The steps she took to perpetuate this crime were cunning, even though not brilliant.

There were too many planned steps to consider this an impetuous crime. It was calculated: the renting of the apartment under the false name, a welfare application where she described herself as being pregnant, and her description at the bank on the 17th of December when she said she was employed at the hospital as a registered nurse. On the 18th of December as earlier indicated, she purchased clothing for a baby girl. On the 22nd, she inquired about purchasing baby clothes and furniture. On the 23rd prior to the kidnapping, she purchased baby clothes. She used surgical gloves when she was in the room which, to me, would indicate that she was aware of the fact that she might leave fingerprints. She has a familiarity with hospitals generally, and obviously, with that hospital specifically. The hair dye, as I have earlier indicated, was for no other purpose but to disguise her appearance so that she wouldn't be apprehended. All of these acts are consistent with a calculated and intentional planned kidnapping of a baby girl. I am sure that it was not intended that it be Shelby, but it was intended that it be a baby girl from the Joseph Brant Hospital.

I accept that she has been abused emotionally and perhaps physically by her common law husband. I accept her remorse. I accept that she must be given consideration for a plea of guilty at the earliest opportunity, although, as the Crown has pointed out, the evidence against her was overwhelming. Notwithstanding that, I still consider that she ought to be given consideration for the fact of the early plea of guilty. Notwithstanding all of the mitigating factors, I cannot disregard the enormity of this crime, not only the effect that it has had on the Walsh family, but the effect that such a crime has had on this community, this province, this country. That is what criminal laws are designed to protect against. A sentence to be imposed must be denunciatory of such conduct. I believe that seven years is at the lower, if not the lowest, end of an appropriate range of sentence for this crime. Your sentence will be seven years imprisonment.

Gasps and whispers are heard as the sentence is read.

In addition, the law requires that you be prohibited from possessing firearms, ammunition or explosives and that will be for a period of ten years after your release from prison.

Before closing, I want to thank both counsels for the very professional way that they have handled this case and presented their submissions. Obviously, the speed with which this case was dealt, less than three months from the date of the crime, is reflective of the co-operation that both the counsel, and for that matter, the accused, has exhibited in disposing of this very tragic matter.

The judge looks at the convicted criminal and closes by saying, "I wish you well in serving your sentence and I hope that in the future with counselling and treatment you will never again find yourself acting so despicably irresponsible as you did on this occasion."

The media in the courtroom cannot approach us during the trial. They watch closely and observe from afar. Emotions run high when the judge reads the sentence. I cover my face with my hands and cry. There are so many feelings running through me: relief, sadness, and validation. My tears run freely. Our friends from the police department move in closer, and like a cloak they shelter us from the storm of onlookers — one of them hands me a Kleenex. Words cannot explain the relationship we have developed with these people. The experience we have shared with them is so intimate that they feel like part of our family. There is no one I would rather have beside me, not only *by* my side but *on* my side.

We stay in the courtroom until everyone has left. We take the time to discuss the sentencing and then go to the Crown attorney's office to speak to Richard Garwood-Jones. When I see him we impulsively embrace and it feels right and good. There is a feeling of jubilation in the small office. Richard Garwood-Jones has set precedence with this case, and he has much to be proud of. We say goodbye to him and attempt to thank him, but the words don't do justice. There is no way to convey how appreciative we are.

We make our way outside to the barrage of people waiting to hurl questions. On the steps of the courthouse, the press cameras and microphones come out for the media scrum.

"What did you think of the verdict?"

"Were you satisfied with the judge's sentence?"

"What did you think of the judge's statement that this was a heinous crime?"

We answer all the questions as the cameras roll and the pencils scribble. Finally, we are free to go and start our lives again. It is time to put all of this behind us.

The next day, every newspaper distributed in our area has a story about the trial. Typical front-page photographs show us on the courthouse steps, answering questions. Pictures of the now-convicted kidnapper also fill the paper, accompanied by excerpts of an interview with her shortly after the sentencing, in which she says,

> I think the sentence was extremely stiff, and the judge is making an example of me. I think he based it mainly on the mother's testimony. I mean I'm losing so many things! I'm not going to see my grandson. I probably won't see him grow up nor see my parents alive again. There are a lot of people out there who have committed terrible crimes. They're getting two years less a day, over and over and over again. Even repeat offenders and men who rape children are still not getting real, federal penitentiary time.

The police take the kidnapper off to jail to serve her sentence. From there she pens a letter that we receive shortly after. It opens with a math equation and a question: "11 hours = 7 years?" The letter continues, expressing her dissatisfaction with the sentence and her general disdain toward us. The anonymous letter remains unsigned, but handwriting analysis indicates that she is the author, confirming what we already suspected: the letter read by the kidnapper in court was a ruse. There is no regret. There is no shame. There is no conscience.

The police suggest that if we receive any further anonymous mail to leave it unopened and call them. A week later we receive a second letter, and we open it as we have been instructed not to do.

The correspondence is once again from the kidnapper. We call the police and they once again retrieve the letter. The authorities explain to the convicted woman the ramifications of continuing to contact us. Both letters are now in the possession of the legal system. No more letters have arrived.

| EPILOGUE |

One Year Later

After the resolution to Shelby's kidnapping, everyone, including me, expected life to go on as usual. Everyone expected me to be fine, and when anyone asked how I was, I would say, "I'm fine." I wasn't fine. I must have heard a hundred times how we had experienced a happy ending and we must be thrilled. But life doesn't come in shades of black and white. It's all grey. Anyone who has gone through a catastrophic event will tell you that you relive the whole gamut of emotions that made up the experience, over and over again. I couldn't understand or justify my distress. Like asthma, my suffering was invisible to everyone but me.

I was diagnosed as suffering from post-traumatic stress disorder (PTSD). PTSD can be caused by virtually any event that is life-threatening or by any event that severely threatens your emotional well-being. People who have gone through a severe accident can experience PTSD. Many soldiers returning from war suffer from PTSD. Support workers during war, such as nurses, doctors, and journalists, have experienced PTSD — they didn't carry weapons but they fought a battle. The danger is passed, but the effects of the experience linger.

Though it is just a title, it validated that I wasn't crazy, that there was an actual medical condition to describe what I was going through. The symptoms of PTSD included everything I had been experiencing: Flashbacks became part of my daily experience and recurring nightmares part of my evenings. Problems sleeping contributed to trouble concentrating.

I had a tendency to be startled and had a hypervigilance to threat. My senses triggered fear before I could rationalize why. The smell of antiseptic, the sight of a hospital, the sound of a siren or simply feet walking down the hall, the touch of a stranger looking over my shoulder to sneak a look at my newborn — all these things and many more were a source of alarm. It was easier to avoid places, people, and experiences that were a reminder of the trauma.

My mind became a sentry, protecting, monitoring, and shielding me from memories that were shocking. Like my brother after my father's death, I had my hand on a doorknob and I knew there was something terrible on the other side. I couldn't open that door. I tried to remember, but the door was locked. As was typical of PTSD, I experienced blackouts and memory impairment. The retrieving of memory was indiscriminate, and it was not just memories trauma-related that were blocked — any memory at all was suddenly just out of my reach, and my inability to recall even current events became a constant source of embarrassment to me.

I talked to a therapist, as did some of the nurses who were on staff at the hospital during the kidnapping. They also struggled with the after-effects of the kidnapping and suffered from PTSD. These health care workers were the forgotten victims of the crime. They were never recognized or mentioned as being affected by the events of that day, but they suffered greatly. Some received counselling and others went about their lives, carrying secret wounds that would never fully heal. Everyone probably thought that they would be fine.

I have seen many people judged by their community while going through public ordeals, such as when their children go missing or lose their life tragically. Inevitably, someone will voice their suspicions and judgements that "the mother looks too calm," or "they are not even upset, they should be showing more signs of duress." There are no guidelines on the proper behaviour during times of great loss. Everyone grieves and copes differently, and there is no start and finish line. The struggle for peace of mind is never-ending.

Two years after my daughter was kidnapped, my dear friend Annie's ex-husband picked up their children for a scheduled visit. Unbeknownst to her, it would be the last time she would ever see them alive. He drove around until the children fell asleep and then pulled into a storage unit he had rented earlier in the day. He shut the garage door, got back in the car, and left it running until the gas ran out. Her children were the same age as mine, seven and nine. Annie lived for two weeks not knowing where her children were, or what her husband had done to them, and himself. When a child perishes, there is more than one death — surviving loved ones die in a way that can't be put to words. The people left behind live a life filled with questions. What age would that child be now, what would they look like, what would they be doing, what if the circumstances had been different?

Annie survived the nightmare. Like an accident victim who had lost a limb, she made a new life for herself. In her case she was missing a part of her heart and soul. Like many survivors of trauma, the one suffering may appear fine on the outside, but the public doesn't see how she grieves in private. A person never recovers from an ordeal of that magnitude. How could they? Annie continues to live her life with unfailing strength, dignity, and grace. She has been an inspiration to me during many periods of my life. To this day, I feel Annie is the only one who understands why I have such trouble remembering things. Annie and I often joke about our inability to recall information. We both carry a pen and paper for important details, which is not much help when you forget where you put the paper or what the scribbled words were supposed to remind you of. Annie recently relocated and I have been to her house on many occasions, yet it is a standing joke that I will call her just before I leave and ask her where she lives. I truly don't remember.

I have spoken to women like Annie who have gone through unspeakable loss, and they have told me, "I want to be happy, but I'm not happy. I want to be fine, but I'm not fine." We put great pressure on ourselves to remain stoic in times of crisis, and yet true strength perhaps comes from having the courage to be human and wear your heart on your sleeve.

A year after the kidnapping, the interest in our story had not diminished. Portfolio Entertainment produced a movie of the week titled *Stolen Miracle*, which was based on our story, and the cast included Leslie Hope, Dean McDermott, and a young Michael Cera. There were many people who wanted to interview us for various documentaries and talk shows.

We declined participation in several talk shows until we received a call from the *Leeza* show. The producer was very persuasive. "Wouldn't you like to take your family on a vacation? … Wouldn't you like to help other woman avoid what happened to you? You could help to educate the public.

"Wouldn't you like to meet someone else who has gone through the same situation as you? We have two other women who have agreed to come on the show, and you could talk to them about your experience."

Bingo. The magic words were "someone who has gone through what you have."

Leeza was a mother of young children herself and a person with the compassion to create a facility, Leeza's Place, which provides support for family caregivers of loved ones with any chronic illness or disease.

We agreed to travel to Hollywood, California, to attend the *Leeza* show as guests, along with two other mothers whose children had been kidnapped and eventually rescued.

The first woman, Patricia, also had her child kidnapped from her hospital room. The child was eleven hours old. There were a lot of similarities between our stories. Patricia's baby's kidnapper had dressed up as a nurse, even told the mother her baby was anaemic and that she had to take her for blood work. The nurse imposter said she'd be back in a couple of minutes and gave the mother a beeper, instructing her to come and get the baby if it went off. The mother thought it odd that the nurse left with the baby in her arms, but she didn't question her. When the real nurse came back, she asked the mother where her child was, and the mother told her a nurse had taken her for blood work. The real nurse looked at the empty bassinet and inquired, "Without this?"

The kidnapper's demise came when the beeper was traced back to her boyfriend. The boyfriend was in jail, and when visited by the police, he told the investigators his wife had just left with their baby. The investigation showed that the woman visiting her husband had not given birth. The kidnapper was eventually caught, enabling the true mother to be reunited with her daughter.

The second mother, Terri, also had her baby kidnapped from a hospital room. The child was three months old and was in the pediatric ward being treated for pneumonia. The baby's father had brought in a duffle bag of clothes and left it beside the baby's bed. When the parents left the baby's side for a brief time to go to the cafeteria, they came back to find the baby's bed empty and the intravenous tube lying on the floor. When they asked the nurse where the baby was, she had no idea. Someone had come into the room, put the baby in the duffel bag, and walked out of the hospital. In this case, as in many instances, the FBI did not think the parents were showing appropriate signs of duress and the father went through a two-and-a-half-hour polygraph test before he was eliminated as a suspect.

Their baby was missing for four and a half months. The rescue occurred after a firefighter noticed a woman resembling an artist's sketch of the kidnapper he had seen on the local news. The suspicious woman had a child of the appropriate age with her. The woman was apprehended and the family, who had last seen their child at the age of three months, was reunited with a seven-and-a-half-month-old stranger who didn't recognize his own parents and fought to get out of his mother's arms on the first day she held him.

After taping the show, I spent some time speaking to the other parents. They had also received numerous requests to appear on talk shows. Patricia told me that she had made arrangements to be a guest on the *Oprah* show. Shortly before the program was to be aired, Oprah called Patricia at home to let her know they had decided not to run the show. Oprah, ever conscious of the implications of her actions, was concerned about the danger of not only giving potential kidnappers the idea of stealing a child from the maternity ward of a hospital but also showing people how easy it had been to get away with the crime.

Patricia also recounted a story about Geraldo Rivera planning to have a show about kidnapped children. Rivera had invited a mother Patricia knew to be a guest on his show. Unbeknownst to the mother, he had planned to surprise her by bringing the convicted kidnapper on the stage to sit beside her. I was glad I knew of this story when, a few months later, a producer from *The Geraldo Rivera Show* called me to ask me to be a guest on their program. I told the producer I had heard of the incident with the surprise reunion between mother and kidnapper and that they should be ashamed of themselves.

Terri and her husband, Rob, gave me their phone number. As the paper with contact information changed hands, Terri said to me, "We've had seven years to heal. I think I know what you're going through. If you ever want to talk...."

When, years after the event, I was still confused by my inability to feel like my old self again, I gave them a call. When Rob answered, I told him who I was and that I was taking them up on their offer to talk. He couldn't have been nicer. He told me how for years they struggled with the whole situation, and he shared some of the problems that they had getting over it. He said that after about three years they finally found their peace.

"... How?" I asked.

"We forgave."

Yeah, like that's ever gonna happen. "Any other advice?"

I could hear the smile in his response. "I know it sounds unfathomable, but until you can forgive her and let it go, you are never going to find peace."

He wished me well and handed the phone off to his wife. I expected her to respond, "Men, what do they know," but instead she reiterated what he had said. She had found her peace and had moved on. She would never forget. She would never condone. She still grieved, but she had forgiven and that was what had saved her.

We talked some more about the struggles and fears of the real world. That was the last time I ever spoke to her. She had good advice but I wasn't ready for it. I wasn't ready to feel good yet.

Ironically, on the same day, I also received a letter from a boy I went to school with in the primary grades and hadn't spoken to since I was a child. Interestingly, the people I thought I would hear from after the kidnapping were not the ones that called. The people I would have never expected to hear from were the ones that reached out to me by phone and correspondence. Life is full of surprises. Jimmy, who now referred to himself as James, wrote an eloquent letter saying how he and his wife had prayed for me when they heard of the kidnapping and that they hoped I would find peace in faith and forgiveness. It touched me greatly that he reached out to me, but I wasn't able to take his advice.

I felt giving forgiveness was like saying, "What you did is acceptable." It would no longer make me a victim and I would have no reason to be upset. Forgiveness was the furthest thing from my mind. I would never go there. I would never give her that absolution. What I didn't know was that I was only hurting myself.

Four Years Later

For the first four years of Shelby's life, she was never out of my sight. Even when I was inside the house, she never left my side. If I went into the kitchen to make dinner, she sat on the counter beside me. While doing the laundry, she would sit on top of the dryer while I was filling the washing machine and sit on the washing machine when the time came to move the clothes to the dryer. The whole time she remained happy as a lark, chatting away while she swung her little feet. When I tucked her into bed, I sat in her room until she fell asleep. If she was in another room with her brother or sister, I would call out to them for continual updates.

Her brother and sister were not immune to my hypervigilance. Some of the parents of their friends were not impressed by my questions before leaving them at their houses. If I didn't think it was safe or the parents weren't conscientious enough, the children were not allowed to go to events. Questioning another person's parenting is not a great way to make friends.

When Shelby had to start school, I was a nervous wreck. For the first time, her safety would be in someone else's hands and out of my control. I went to the doctor. "Shelby starts school tomorrow and I feel like I am going to have a meltdown. Would you prescribe me five days' worth of tranquilizers? Just five days to get me through the first week. Surely after five days I won't be so strung out."

I repeated the number five so many times I felt like the Count on *Sesame Street*. What if I liked the pills? What if they made me feel so much better that I wanted them all the time? Seeing my father's addiction had made me wary of drugs and alcohol. Better stick to five days' worth. The doctor understood. She was the same physician who had delivered Shelby, and she knew how hard I had been struggling.

The medication was not enough to calm my fears. I dropped Shelby off at school for her first day of classes and felt the overwhelming fear and panic taking over. I figured if I could exhaust myself with activity I would be able to relax, so I climbed on my bicycle and rode up the Niagara Escarpment — a landmark that is accessible by many steep hills in our area. I rode for hours, until I was so exhausted I was ready to drop. It helped, but it was difficult to keep up on a daily basis. Frustration and anger accompanied my fear. Bitterness grew from my continued resentment toward the kidnapper, and it was exhausting.

Troubles are like the days of the week — we have to go through every one of them, but the weekend eventually comes. I can't say when I turned the corner. It was a gradual process that I didn't embrace, but one that I accepted slowly and begrudgingly. One day, I went for a long run and thought about this place I was stuck in. Instead of remembering song lyrics to escape what was bothering me, I faced the idea of absolution. Perhaps grace was a possibility. I tried out some words that I never thought would pass my lips: "I forgive you." I said them out loud — tentatively, quietly. It didn't feel bad at all. Quite the opposite. A heaviness lifted, and I tried it again, louder and with more conviction, "I forgive you," and at that moment in time I turned a corner, literally and figuratively. I smiled. I was free.

I have learned a forgiveness that I can live with. I recognize a wrong was committed, but I will not waste any more negative energy focusing on the event. The hate I was carrying in my heart was a vial of poison that was steadily releasing into my system and sapping the life from me. I took my life back — it was mine to claim right from the start.

Since the kidnapping there have been some positive changes. There is improved security in the hospital maternity wards and advanced training for hospital staff and parents. Despite these advances, parents should feel empowered to question protocol. Instincts should always be followed, and there is no offence in questioning an authority figure. There is a certain sense of transparency in the Canadian health care system and holding hospital staff accountable to their actions is more important than worrying about hurting anyone's feelings.

My story is unique but my challenges are not. We have all struggled with fear, sadness, anger, confusion, and pain. It's okay to feel these emotions; they are all part of the human condition, but there comes a time to move on. The past is just that — something better left behind. There's no sense looking over my shoulder when there is so much to look forward to.

I can't say that we live in a perfect world, but I can say one thing, and of this I am sure: Sometimes, bad things happen. More often, good things happen. Life is a series of hurdles, but the straightaway is always longer than that jump.

It doesn't matter who our father or mother is, where we're from, how we grew up, whether or how we were wronged. We are responsible for our life. It is up to us to decide what we want to dwell on in our past and whether we want to be a victim or a victor. We can spend our life rehashing every bad thing that ever happened to us, guaranteeing a future of pain and sorrow, or we can base our life on the happy and beautiful moments that we choose to revisit. We can thread them together like a string of Christmas bulbs and light them daily in celebration of life. I choose to flip the switch on happiness. I choose to count my blessings. I deserve to be happy, we all do.

Fifteen Christmases Later

It is Christmas Day by one hour. I am looking over at Shelby. She is wedged between her brother and sister — three people squeezed into a loveseat made for two. They are each sipping on a margarita in a salt-rimmed glass and looking at the Christmas book. We are just home from the traditional Christmas Eve celebration at my brother Chuck's house.

The Christmas book is a photographic journey that chronicles the last three decades of Christmases. As they reminisce about uncles, aunts, grandparents, and friends, the three siblings joke and laugh. Their laughter is music to my ears, and their closeness feels more intoxicating than any cocktail. I say the names of my children in my head and send up an unspoken thank you.

Shelby once said to me, "You say my name differently than anyone else."

I thought about what she said and listened to how other people pronounced her name. What I realized was that it was not just the pronunciation that was different, it was the emotion threaded through the letters. When we say our children's names, you can actually hear the love and adoration coming from our lips.

I look at my son. He is a man now, but I still see the boy he once was. The curve of his jaw, the smirk, the blond cowlick in his hair, the laughter and glance he throws his sisters' way are still the same as when he was young. The boy who couldn't put down his pencil and sketched constantly has graduated with his B.A. in illustration. The boy who left his comic books all over the house has now written his own graphic novel. The boy who never stopped singing is now strumming his guitar and composing his own music. The boy who watched over his little sisters is now a man who still looks out for their well-being.

I see my oldest daughter, my Beauty. She is a woman now, but I still see the girl she once was. At the nape of her neck, where her blond tendrils curve around her collar, I still see the little girl who I would help with her shampoo; funny, loving, intelligent, and strong, she was a leader from the start. She is now three-quarters nurse, doing her internship in Labour and Delivery — a fitting profession for a child who was always very intuitive and expressive.

She could always pick out the one person at a gathering who looked in need of help. She would say things like, "Mommy, that girl in the corner is very sad." I would look over and wonder how I had missed what she had so easily observed.

Shelby.

My Shelby, my Angel — I say her name in reverence; I say her name like a benediction. Not a day goes by that I don't give thanks for the safe return of this child. She is the final piece of our family. She is now in high school and a happy, confident young woman. She sleeps under a blanket of love, a quilt made from cut up pieces of her baby clothes and my maternity wear, stitched together with thread and memories.

She loves animals, especially her Jack Russell terrier, Max. After it rains, she moves the snails from the walkway to the garden so that they don't get stepped on. Her favourite foods include avocados, mangoes, and pork and beans, but without the pork because "pigs are smart." She has a laugh that's contagious and tears that could break your heart. Her wardrobe includes vintage belts, homemade socks, Converse high-top running shoes and well-worn Doc Martens. Dresses hang in her closet, Steve Madden heels sit on her floor, and beads hang from her jewellery tree. She loves camping, bonfires, fireworks, and a night at the theatre. She loves old movies and music from all genres. She knows the entire soundtrack from the movies *The Sound of Music*, *White Christmas*, and *Oliver Twist*, and her music preferences range anywhere from The Beatles to Weezer. She is a bibliophile and savours a new book almost as much as she loves chocolate.

She has no memory of what happened to her. She was not traumatized by her kidnapping but has been aware of how the rest of us have coped with it over the years. Perhaps because of her early and first-hand education in the effects of trauma, she is very conscious of the plight of others. She is a human rights advocate and a graduate of the Asper Foundation Human Rights and Holocaust Studies program. She is very sensitive to the injustices in our society toward various ethnic, racial, and religious groups, through prejudice, and on the largest possible scales such as in Nazi-occupied Europe, Rwanda, and Darfur, Sudan. She knows that knowledge is power and that we must use that knowledge to end injustices.

People often ask me when and how Shelby learned of the kidnapping. We never had the opportunity to choose when to share Shelby's story with her, and she has known since she was old enough to comprehend adult conversation. People have asked us questions and freely discussed the kidnapping in front of Shelby since the day she came home from the hospital. She has always known that she was Baby Shelby, that child that was kidnapped.

We never hid the details of the kidnapping — we also did not discuss them. It was an ordeal we kept to ourselves. I have questioned whether I should open up this door to the past and invite it into the present. Openly discussing my past has caused discomfort for some of my loved ones, and for that I am sorry. In the end I had to be true to myself, and acknowledging the truth has been essential for me to heal.

We have remained friends with the police officers, detectives, and sergeants that we met over the course of events. They attended Shelby's baptism, as did the lawyer, Richard Garwood-Jones. I think of these people often and fondly, particularly as we go through the different milestones in Shelby's life.

I think back over the journey we have all travelled and I count my blessings.

This Christmas my heart overflows with joy. "If I could save time in a bottle," I would capture this moment and store it with all of the other wonderful times in my life.

Every night when I lay my head down on the pillow I give thanks. Every morning when I wake up I give thanks again and I hope. I hope that I can instill in my children an everlasting optimism and belief in themselves and the good of mankind. I hope that every day they feel gratitude for the abundance that surrounds them and for this unpredictable and mysterious thing we call life.

A Note from Shelby

At sixteen years old, I have a lot of memories. I remember what it was like to be on stage in the school play, and I remember the first time I had a banana split. There is also a lot that I don't remember, like what I had for breakfast last Tuesday. I also don't remember being taken from my mother's arms and coming unsettlingly close to having lived a completely different life, raised by a shadow instead of by the wonderful angels that I call my Mum and Dad.

During my first year of high school, a kidnapping with circumstances very similar to mine happened in Sudbury, Ontario. Afterwards, reporters came knocking on our door again and the kids at school began to ask me questions about my own kidnapping. The most commonly asked question by both reporters and classmates was, "Do you think that the kidnapping affected your childhood and the way that you grew up?"

This question never came as a surprise to me, but it always left me wondering. At first I thought it was silly. My immediate response was that of course I grew up normally, there was nothing different about my childhood compared to anyone else's. The more I thought about it, though, the more I realized that I didn't have a normal childhood — I had one that was better than normal.

Having what I felt was a very overprotective mother was actually beneficial to me. Well, not overprotective ... let's just say thorough. My friends became very accustomed to my Mum and Dad's ways. When I was very young, it began with my mother calling my name. I would say, "Yes, Mum?" and she would respond with a sentence that quickly became the most repeated phrase of my childhood, "Just wondering where you are."

My mother became well acquainted with all the parents of my elementary school friends so that she could trust them to look after me when I went to their houses for play dates. As I grew older, I became very familiar with every safety rule in the book:

wear a helmet when riding a bike, always stay on the main roads, never go anywhere alone, don't talk to strangers. Then there were the adolescent rules: never leave your drink out of sight, never go to the bathroom alone, and never leave the building you are in at nighttime, especially in unfamiliar neighbourhoods.

On significant outings my mother would request to speak with the parent of the kids who were also involved, and if it was a school trip, she would come along as a volunteer. There were numerous ways in which my parents have ensured that nothing bad will ever happen to me — nothing bad that can be prevented, anyways. I don't have memories of my dad being quite as vigilant as my mom was, but I've come to the conclusion that it was because she was always thorough enough for the both of them. By the time she was done checking out the situation, there was nothing left for him to ask.

The way that my household was when my siblings and I were growing up never bothered me. I never really realized that it was different than other households in the first place. Every home and family is different, and my house was different in a way that I came to love and cherish. How could I dislike a household who loved me so much that all they wanted to do was try to keep me safe? How could I dislike a household with siblings who enjoyed spending time with one another? How could I dislike a household that was absolutely full of optimism and encouragement and always remained positive, despite the hardship they had been through? I like the way I grew up, and I love the people that I grew up with. My dad, my mom, my brother, and my sister are the most important people in my life. They have positively influenced me and they have comforted me.

In my opinion, most things happen for a reason. Even in the worst situations, you can always find something good that happened because of something bad. I've spent some time thinking about the different ways that my life and the lives of the people closest to me could have turned out had the kidnapping ended with a different outcome, or had a different baby been kidnapped. But it didn't end with a different outcome, and I was the one taken. It ended in the best possible way that it could have. Whether you believe in God or in the Force or in power of positive thinking, I believe that something special happened the day that I was kidnapped. So many people were praying and hoping, so many were wishing for a happy ending. I have to believe that there was some power in all of that positive energy, and when I was rescued it gave people something to believe in.

Although the kidnapping seemed awful at the time, I think that things happened exactly as they were supposed to, and that in the end it was of benefit. My mom is such a positive person and my dad is such a strong person, both physically, with rock-solid arms, and emotionally, in a way that I will always admire. I see the kidnapping not as a bad thing that happened to me and my family but as something that contributed to the way we are now. If it hadn't happened, we wouldn't be the same people. I wouldn't be the same person, and I wouldn't want to be a person who never understood pain or hardship. I wouldn't want to be a person who couldn't appreciate the amazing things that I have. I want to wake up and realize that there is always something to appreciate, something to be thankful for, something to smile about, even in the worst of times. I am so thankful for the things that I have and the people in my life. I can even find some thanks that the kidnapping happened, because it is part of what made me who I am today.

The Shadow and Others

Karen Susan Hill pled guilty and in February 1994 was convicted of kidnapping. She was awarded a seven-year sentence. It was thought she would be eligible for parole in July of 1996, but spokesman for Immigration Canada Kevin Sack reported that Hill was found to be a danger to the public and was refused parole. Hill also lost her right to appeal. Sack said Hill's landed immigrant status was revoked and she would receive orders to be deported when released from prison.

Police said Hill, whose sentence expired in June 2001, also faced weapons charges in Oklahoma and fraud offences in Michigan.

Sergeant Ansell was able to go home and tell her children that she found the baby. She is now divorced and no longer working for the police department — she went back to school and is now a registered nurse. Detective Peron is married with a family of his own and has transferred to a different division. Sergeant Ford is now retired from the police department.

One of the cashiers at the pharmacy won the lottery, as did one of the police officers who helped in the investigation.

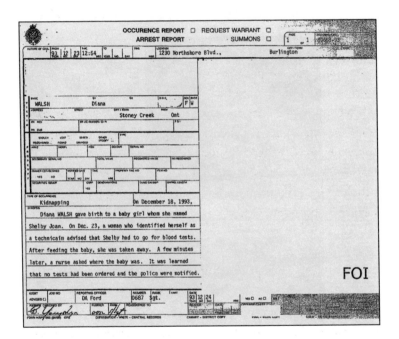

Merry Christmas
THE TORONTO STAR

Light snow. High -6C   **Friday, December 24, 1993**   Ontario Edition

STAR
SANTA
CLAUS
FUND
TARGET $900,000
COLLECTED $743,638

Girls, 6, sell their drawings for Santa fund

BY MARK ZWOLINSKI
STAFF REPORTER

It's never too late to be like Santa Claus.

Or like Melissa Rourke.

The call goes out as agencies labor to needy children the few boxes provided by The Star Santa Claus Fund.

The Christmas spirit may be warming our homes today, but the fund is still well short of the $900,000 it needs to help some 45,000 children across Metro and you may still donate.

To picture, A4

The fund will be extended past its Christmas deadline.

Those kids will have at least a present to open — a gift stuffed with warm clothing, candy, and a toy — thanks to your donations.

But this season we need just a little extra push to reach the finish line.

The kind of push that comes from someone like Melissa.

The 6-year-old Mississauga girl pranced through the bitter cold night air Wednesday on a door-to-door mission to help her $30 for the fund.

She was canvassing her neighborhood intent on selling her own hand-drawn pictures. A thermometer had dropped one of its lowest levels this year and a fresh blanket of new made sidewalks icy.

But in this battle against Old Man Winter, the old man lost.

"I was freezing, but she didn't it at all, she was just running from door to door," said Melissa's mom, Laurie, who accompanied her daughter on her

☞ Please see Still, A12

Police hunt 5-day-old baby snatched from hospital bed

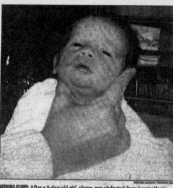

SEEKING CLUES: After a 5-day-old girl, above, was abducted from her mother's room at Burlington's Joseph Brant Hospital, police immediately began a frantic search. OPP Constable Vince Arienna, below, looks in the trunk of a car.

RICHARD LAUTENS / TORONTO STAR

BY PRIMJO GOMBU
AND PETER EDWARDS
STAFF REPORTERS

BURLINGTON — Halton police launched a massive search yesterday after a 5-day-old girl was snatched from Joseph Brant Memorial Hospital.

A short, husky woman between 45 and 50 years old apparently took Baby Shelby from the hospital's temporary maternity ward at about 1 p.m.

The woman, about 5 feet 4 inches tall, was dressed in what resembled a nurse's uniform — blue smock, white pants and white shoes, said Halton Region police Sergeant Joe Martin.

The woman, who has a round face and dark, slightly curly hair, "knew what she was doing," he added.

Shelby's parents and other family members were at the hospital yesterday as at least 30 police officers — including members of the major crime squad — combed the building for the six-pound baby.

"There has been no such occurrence before (in the region) and the parents are extremely distraught," Martin said. "This is a nightmare. God only knows the reason.

"It could be a black market thing or maybe a woman with psychological problems who had a baby that didn't live."

Police have only released the baby's first name. The family has not been identified but police said they are from Stoney Creek, near Hamilton. The mother is in her late 20s and has other children.

A total of 16 detectives and 30 uniformed officers from across the region have been assigned to the case. Police were searching door-to-door in the area last night.

All regional police offices and border crossings have been alerted, Martin said.

Shelby could be far away, police said after a five-hour search.

"She could be as far away as North Bay if (the woman is) driving and if she's taking a plane she could be a lot farther," said Staff Sergeant Boris Yacyshyn of Halton police.

Police were "satisfied she's gone" after a top-to-bottom search of the hospital and its grounds ended in darkness during the supper hour, Yacyshyn said.

Police are reviewing videotape from seven security cameras mounted at the hospital's entrances and exits.

The incident shocked staff and patients, winding down for the Christmas holidays at the hospital.

"I feel sick," said hospital spokesperson Bruce Jackson. "We were looking forward to a season of joy and happiness and now we're stuck with this."

Shelby, who has light blond hair, was healthy when she disappeared from her mother's bedside around 1 p.m. yesterday.

She had been kept in the hospital to comfort her mother, who had suffered complications in the birth. The woman and her baby were to have been released yesterday.

There were some parents in her room along with at least two other babies, Martin said. The ward was temporarily set aside for maternity patients because the hospital is undergoing major renovations.

The woman in the light blue smock made "idle conversation" with the other women before approaching the mother, he said.

The mother didn't suspect anything was wrong when the woman said she was taking Shelby for blood tests, Jackson said.

But nursing staff became frantic minutes later, when they

☞ Please see Baby, back page

Cover of the Toronto Star *December 24, 1993.*

Cover of the Toronto Sun *December 24, 1993.*

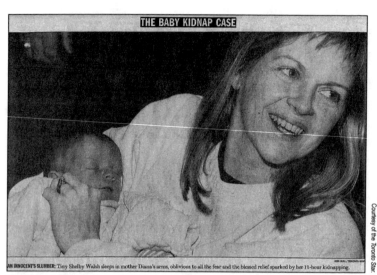

THE BABY KIDNAP CASE

AN INNOCENT'S SLUMBER: Tiny Shelby Walsh sleeps in mother Diana's arms, oblivious to all the fear and the blessed relief sparked by her 11-hour kidnapping.

RON BULL / TORONTO STAR

Courtesy of the Toronto Star.

The Baby Kidnap Case.

Luck & leg work

Finding baby Shelby was 'a miracle' police say

By STEVE ARNOLD and BELINDA SUTTON
The Spectator

SHEER LUCK and hours of leg work are what returned baby Shelby Walsh to her mother's arms, say the two Halton police officers who found her.

Detective-Sergeant Lee-Ann Ansell and Detective-Constable Chris Perrin discovered the five-day-old baby in a Burlington motel room Thursday evening about 11 hours after she was abducted from Joseph Brant Memorial Hospital.

Sgt. Ansell pulled back a blanket on an unmade bed and discovered the newborn sound asleep.

Ansell

■ **Woman acted oddly: A2**

"I cried," said Sgt. Ansell, a police officer for almost 12 years. "I was really happy and excited and I cried."

Sgt. Ansell and Const. Perrin were part of a massive hunt organized to find the infant after she was taken from her mother's room at the hospital, where she was born.

The two detectives decided to

Perrin

check out motels on Plains Road East after interviewing two cashiers, employed by a nearby Big V Drug Store, at their homes. The women reported seeing a customer at the store who matched the description of the woman suspected of taking the child.

The Town & Country Motel was the second one checked. A couple managing the motel said no one matching the description was staying there.

Const. Perrin, a police officer for almost seven years, asked if any women had recently checked in. The couple said there was one, whom they thought had stayed there before.

The officers went to Room 130. When a woman opened the door, the officers were stunned. She exactly matched witnesses' description of the suspect.

"I looked at Lee-Ann and our jaws dropped," Const. Perrin, 29, said.

The woman, clad in a housecoat and nightie, appeared nervous and asked what the officers wanted and why they were there.

"I told her it was really cold out – could we come in and talk to her for a moment?" Const. Perrin said. "She was a bit hesitant, but she allowed us to come in."

Once inside, Const. Perrin noticed clothing and other items described by the Big V cashiers on one of the beds.

"We noticed the other bed was a little bit unmade, but both pillows were showing and there was a little bit of a lump on the bed underneath the covers."

The detectives chatted with the woman for several minutes before Const. Perrin managed to distract her. As he did, Sgt. Ansell pulled back the covers on the unmade bed and found the missing infant.

"I couldn't believe it," Const. Perrin said. "It was a miracle. It really was."

Const. Perrin immediately arrested the woman

□ Continued on A2

Mathew McCarthy, Special to The Spectator

Five-day-old Shelby Walsh is back safe in the arms of mother Diana and father Glenn.

Courtesy of the Hamilton Spectator.

Front page of the Hamilton Spectator, *December 27, 1993.*

Artist's sketch of the kidnapper.

Police unit honored for work

Baby Shelby found safe and sound thanks to team spirit

The Halton police team which found kidnapped baby Shelby Walsh in a Burlington motel Dec. 23 was honored by its commander at a recent police commission meeting.

Insp. Les Graham, chief of the major crimes bureau, officially tipped his hat to the 25-member investigative unit, but singled out six officers in particular:

Sgt. Lee Ann Ansell and Det.-Const. Chris Perrin, in checking hotels on Burlington's Plains Road, discovered the baby after gaining entry to a motel room.

Ansell found baby Shelby under blankets on a bed while Perrin distracted the woman. The baby was not injured.

"They knocked on the door of a female occupant at the Town and Country motel and used their street smarts to gain entry," said Graham.

Det. Doug Ford of the major crimes unit was chief investigator during the incident and tirelessly gathered background necessary to the upcoming court case.

Det. Dale Stanton and Det. Const. Mike Demeester conducted a series of interviews crucial to the case.

"Three of the interviews they conducted were of a highly sensitive nature, and were necessary in solving the case," said Graham.

It took a team effort to bring baby Shelby Walsh back to her parents, Diana and Glenn, centre. Hal Police officers, who played roles in that effort, left to right, are: Det.-Const. Chris Perrin, Sgt. L Stanton, Det.-Const. Mike Demeester, Sgt. Lee Ann Ansell, Const. John Wolak, Det. Doug Ford Acting Insp. Mike Eacrett.

Sgt. Joe Martin, of the force's media relations unit, was recognized for volunteering his vacation time to come in and handle the heavy media coverage.

Martin travelled from his Brampton home a number of times over the two-day period to keep the press up-to-date on the investigation, said Graham.

Halton Police Chief Peter

Campbell also praised the unit.

"There was some good ingenuity from the police officers involved. They demonstrated everything that is right in our society," said Campbell.

Shelby was found Dec. 23, 11 hours after she was abducted from Joseph Brant Memorial Hospital.

The baby was five days old at

the time of her kidnapping.

Karen Susan Hill, 48, is char; with kidnapping. She is be held at the Hamilton-Wentwc Detention Centre and will g trial by judge alone tomorr (Monday) at the Milton co house.

The Halton police team responsible for finding Baby Shelby

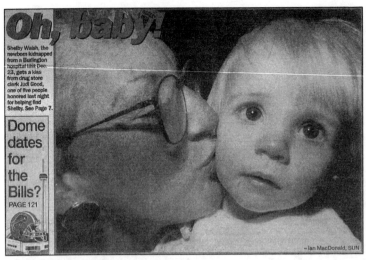

Judi Good kissing Shelby.

A photograph that ran in the Toronto Sun. *The caption read: "Awards: Among those honoured by the Halton Regional Police last night were (from left) Lori Richardson, Kathleen Langdon, and Judith Good. They won the undying gratitude of Diana and Glenn Walsh (right), parents of 11-month-old Shelby being carried by her sister Caitlin, 6. The women were instrumental in the return of Shelby, who was abducted from the hospital."*

| Acknowledgements |

This has been a very challenging road to walk, not only for me but for my family. Some have been behind me, encouraging me forward, others, standing quietly on the sidelines and looking the other way. I understand all of their choices and love them for accepting mine.

Thank you, Mom, for your courage and unconditional love; my admiration and respect for you comes only second to my love. Thank you sisters and brother; you will always be my favourite people and the ones I want as members of my club.

Thank you Norma Shephard, Taylor Elson, and Rebecca Antoszek, for your insights.

Thank you to my children for their patience and understanding during the remembering of this event. I adore you and am grateful for your feedback and suggestions.

Thank you to my husband for being my boyfriend, my best friend, and for always walking beside me.

Thank you to my colleagues in my writing group, The North Shore Wordsmiths; I am indebted to you for your sagacity and friendship.

Lastly, thank you to all of the people who helped to reunite me with my daughter. You know who you are. You have given me my life back and I will be forever grateful.

Crime Stoppers: 1-800-222-8477 (TIPS)
Child Find: 1-800-387-7962

Of Related Interest

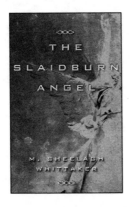

The Slaidburn Angel
M. Sheelagh Whittaker
978-1-459703636
$24.99

While researching her ancestry on the Internet one gloomy evening, Penny is astonished by what she finds. Urgently, she instructs her sister Sheelagh, "Search 'Slaidburn Suspected Child Murder!' Now!" So begins a tragic story within a story spanning more than a century, of the alleged 1885 murder of an illegitimate toddler, unnoticed, unloved, and ultimately left for dead on the bank of a lonely creek in Northern England.

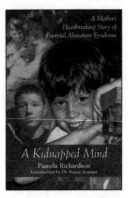

A Kidnapped Mind
A Mother's Heartbreaking Story of Parental Alienation Syndrome
Pamela Richardson
978-1-550026245
$24.99

How do we begin to describe our love for our children? Pamela
Richardson shows us with her passionate memoir of life with
and without her estranged son, Dash. From age five, Dash
suffered Parental Alienation Syndrome at the hands of his father.
Indoctrinated to believe his mother had abandoned him, after years
of monitored phone calls and impeded access, eight-year-old Dash
decided he didn't want to be "forced" to visit her at all; later he told
her he would never see her again if she took the case to court.

A Kidnapped Mind is a heartrending and mesmerizing story
of a Canadian mother's exile from and reunion with her child,
through grief and beyond, to peace.

DUNDURN
www.dundurn.com
Visit us at
Dundurn.com
Definingcanada.ca
@dundurnpress
Facebook.com/dundurnpress